Hold on to
the Messy Times

Myself and my friend and researcher,
Lesley Thomson, whose idea it was that I
write this book. One day I may forgive her!

(photo: *Stewart Rathmill*)

Hold on to
the Messy Times

by SUE JOHNSTON

Research by Lesley Thomson

Illustrations by Kate Charlesworth

PANDORA

London Winchester Sydney Wellington

First published by Pandora Press, an imprint of the Trade Division of
Unwin Hyman, in 1989.

PANDORA PRESS
Unwin Hyman Ltd
15/17 Broadwick Street, London W1V 1FP

Unwin Hyman Inc
8 Winchester Place, Winchester, MA 01890, USA

Allen & Unwin Australia Pty Ltd
PO Box 764, 8 Napier Street, North Sydney, NSW 2060, Australia

Allen & Unwin NZ Ltd (in association with the Port Nicholson Press)
Compusales Building, 75 Ghuznee Street, Wellington 1, New Zealand

British Library Cataloguing in Publication Data

Johnston, Sue, *1943–*
Hold on to the messy times.
1. Great Britain. Acting – Biographies
I. Title
792′.028′0924

Typeset by Wyvern Typesetting Ltd, Bristol
Printed and bound in Great Britain
by Cox & Wyman Limited, Reading

CONTENTS

For my son Joel
And remembering Sarah Ungar and
Michael Hopkin

Acknowledgements

I WOULD LIKE to thank all my friends and colleagues for putting up with me while I was writing this book.

In particular I want to thank Lesley Thomson who guided me and encouraged me and originally came to me with the idea that I could write.

My thanks also to Liverpool football team's John Barnes, whose legs gave me inspiration; to my editor, Philippa Brewster, for her endless support; Frank and Joan Clare; the Coventry Belgrade Theatre in Education team; Anajoy David of Red Wedge; Ric Blaxill and Gary Davies at BBC Radio One; Barbara Jacobs; Paul Jackson of the BBC Information Office; Barbara James at the British Library; Dot Kelly; Mike Kay at the Sheffield Crucible; Debby Klein; Edie McCardle; Len McCormick; Sheila McKechnie, Director of Shelter; Debbie Licorish; Lisa May at *Brookside*; Joyce Molyneaux; Mavis Nicholson; Shirley Noon; Simon Pell and John McTurnan at the Labour Party's Walworth Road headquarters; Irene Pinnington; Sylvia Pye; Phil Redmond and Larry Redmond of *Brookside*; Clare Short, MP; Madge Short; Judy Spiers; Janice Troup of *Brookside*; May Thomson; Vanessa Whitburn of *Brookside*; Dot Wood and the M6 Theatre Company; David Yallop; and last but by no means least, thanks to all my family without whom I would have no stories to tell.

Introduction

I SUPPOSE IT was inevitable that one day someone would ask me to write a book. I could have said no, but the one thing I've been blessed (or cursed) with is the inability to resist a challenge. Then there was the question of what the book should be. I'd always had a temptation to release a Christmas book – 'The Sheila Grant Health and Beauty Book', with a complimentary video and promises to make you into something super-human by sharing the 'secrets of my success'. If I sound cynical, don't get me wrong; I buy them all. And I am still ageing too fast, rather overweight, unfirm, uncon-toured, uncontrolled and spotty.

When I bought these books, apart from trying to find a way to stop the rapid decay of my body, I was looking for help with the increasing number of fears that were creeping into my head. Fear of flying, the loss of my parents, walking alone, sleeping alone, grey hair and bad breath. Fears that I felt silly talking about to my friends. At one point the only way I could stop all these fears taking me over, particularly at night, was to take sleeping pills. These increased my paranoia so much that I spent most of the night wandering round the house, peering out of windows, waiting to be raped and pillaged. Obviously not the woman to preach to anyone about looking thirty for the rest of her life.

So, what to write ... When I was ten I remember watching a black and white 'weepie' about a young girl who desperately wanted to write. 'Only write about what you know', advised the old sage Auntie Somebody-Or-Other. And she did of course, and had a mega best seller, *I Remember Mama*. I then had to have a serious think about what I 'knew'.

What I know is what I've learnt from being little: the good and the bad times, the things I've held on to and stored. The family stories I'd grown up on, about myself and people who had shaped my life. The people I have met who have taught me about things beyond my own experience, like hearing Clare Short say:

'The fact that it is hard is part of it; the messy times we've all been through. If we can hold on to them and admit they happened, and not pretend they didn't, then that in itself makes us bigger.'

I'm happy to have benefited from a questioning mind, and a sometimes dangerous ability to take risks. I have not always come out of them unscathed. Nor, I guess, have the people around me.

In this book there are people, places and events that touched me and moved me and that I have held on to. I hope they will do the same for you. But in the end, though, it's nothing as pompous as that; it's just a book I hope you'll enjoy.

Sue Johnston

'It's funny where you get your bits from': Family

I COME FROM a huge family although I'm an only child. But my mother and father came from big families and they have all been around me from the moment I was born; my mother had five sisters and six brothers. And heading the army, for that's how it seems, were my grandparents, whom I adored. Cousins were like brothers and sisters, aunts and uncles like second mums and dads. Everyone naturally took responsibility for each others' families. My cousin Pauline remembers our Uncle David standing over her while she learned to play the piano, while her father, my Uncle Clyde, stuck my head under the tap to wash off my eye make-up. He said it was far too much for 'a girl of sixteen'. In return, I can remember my own father making Pauline wipe off her lipstick, which he insisted was 'too heavy'.

I was born in my Auntie Milly's house in Warrington; my mother was staying there as my father was away doing his duty for king and country. As sirens wailed and doodle-bugs fell, my aunts snatched me from my mother's arms, and ran with me down to the Anderson shelter in the garden, and safety, leaving my mother to stare at the four walls alone!

I seemed to have so many homes when I was a child: my own near Liverpool, with Auntie May's round the corner, and my two aunts and grandparents in Warrington. Pauline and myself were only a few months apart in age, and Marjorie was a year older. Our young days were spent evenly between all four houses. I've really had the best of both worlds: isolation occasionally, whenever we happened to be in our own home, and the warmth and support of all that extended family.

I grew up on stories, people sitting round telling stories of the past, mainly about the family. The stories about me were always the same; I was the messy one, the dirty one. The one who crawled under train seats and reappeared with cigarette stumps in her mouth or filled her nappy as soon as she had been dressed. Etched in my mind are visions of me as an untidy, filthy child, walking several paces behind a sophisticated mother who was trying to pretend I was nothing to do with her.

I still thrive on these stories, more so nowadays as I grow older and the need to have a sense of my own history becomes vital. My great-grandfather was the station master at Carlisle railway station; he also, with his wife, ran the Globe Hotel, a temperance hotel for commercial travellers in Cumberland. He once had to don a top hat and tails when the then Prince of Wales came through. All ardent royalists, my family must have dined out on that story for years. My grandfather, the son of this barely-glimpsed-at-by-royalty station master, had a nanny and a governess until he was eight years old; he then went on to have a private education. Could it be that my great-grandfather, during that little passing sight of the Prince of Wales, got ideas above his station? That my grandfather ended up working on the railways is a mystery to me, although I suppose driving the *Flying Scotsman* did elevate his position, and it was because his colleagues considered him a snob that they gave him the title of The Duke. One of my fondest memories as a child was riding on this train, and being taken on to the engine when we reached Lime Street station. It was an amazing feeling to know that this powerhouse of machinery was in the control of your own grandfather.

I spent a lot of my childhood at my grandparents' house in Warrington. It was a large house; well it had to be with all those children. It had a big bay window overlooking the main road, the front door was always open, but we never used it, we always used to go round to the backyard. The house formed an L shape around this yard, with the dining room, kitchen and back kitchen windows almost surrounding it. Further on was the garden and a huge washhouse where, as a young-ster, Auntie Ena, kept off school to help her mother, would be up at dawn washing for the family. Outside the washhouse stood a vast, or so it seemed to me, water butt, while propped against the walls were bits of my Dad's old Norton motor bike that he had been forced to abandon under an ultimatum from my mother after several serious accidents. The coal was kept in the corner of the washhouse, piled up high against the wall, almost to the ceiling. And in the opposite corner to this was an old toilet. I loathed using this toilet, and would always try to avoid doing so because it was an ideal home for spiders. I would sit tensely on it ready for sudden flight if I caught sight of one. The other thing I remember about this toilet was the squares of neatly cut newspaper hanging on a string – the original Andrex. I wonder whose job it was to cut the newspapers into such neat, precise squares.

The back door led into the back kitchen. This was purely a functional room, with cooker, storage, and a big stone sink; on top of the cooker, always at the ready, was a gigantic kettle, and at every party or large gathering it was brought out. It held enough water to keep topping up four teapots.

Beyond this was the kitchen, with the big black range where my grandparents used to sit and bicker endlessly. There was a kitchen table where they used to sit and eat endlessly. In the far corner of the room was a huge cupboard with crockery and sewing materials. It also contained all my Grandma's souvenirs, all things she had never been able to part with – another trait I've inherited, I'm sad to say. I used to have to stand precariously on the arm of a chair to dig around in it; it was a treasure trove of excitement for a young girl like me. There were cruets in there, left over from the hotel days, big ones: salt, pepper and mustard with the vinegar in the middle. There were coffee pots and sugar bowls, all pure silver, all with Globe Hotel stamped on the bottom. Higher up I would find the family photograph album, full of faded pictures of faces hardly remembered. But one which I would linger over was of a lady in a crinoline standing in a doorway outside 'Dove Cottage'. Years later I discovered that my great-grandmother's sister was the caretaker of Wordsworth's cottage, and this was a picture of my great-grandmother wearing one of Dorothy Wordsworth's frocks!

To leave the kitchen there was a steep step up to a door, a wooden door, the top half of which was stained glass in dark colours, which opened on to an even darker corridor where the coats and jackets hung. I would close my eyes and run down this corridor, past the coats, past the cupboard under the stairs, which I was convinced was the home of witches and wizards. At the safe end, on the left, there was a dining room and it seemed to me that all it contained was one enormous dining table. It was as if the room was a dining table. It was only ever used on special occasions. Along the wall opposite the window was a long divan that had belonged to my Dad's mother, my Grandma Wright. The end dropped down and my Uncle Charlie, during his courting days with Auntie Barbara, would spend many a night on it, unable to make the long journey home to Birkenhead. My poor Dad, during his courting days with my mother, was allowed no such luxuries. And on many occasions, including some when there was thick snow, would have to walk the twelve miles back to Merseyside after a night on the town. There was a man who must have been in love! I once rather grandly referred to this divan as a *Chaise longue*, only to be immediately put in my place by Auntie Ena:

'*Chaise longue!*', she exclaimed, 'they're only blinking old couches with an end off.'

And then eventually to the last room: the front parlour. This was a big sunny room with a beautiful Victorian fireplace and lots and lots of places to sit. And ornaments, always so many ornaments, bought for Grandma by devoted grandchildren. There were family photographs on the walls. And is it just nostalgia, but was the sun always shining in that room? Upstairs at Grandma's house was always a mystery to me. I stood for hours in the spacious front bedroom trying to work out where all the children had slept. It was only a three-bedroomed house; I never ever saw inside my grand-parents' bedroom. And the remaining bedroom never struck me as being particularly big, at least not big enough for six bouncing boys.

I loved Alfred Cowan, my grandfather. He was a tall, handsome man, quiet, slightly distant and, when he did talk to you, he had that wonderful quality of making you feel extremely special. My own father and my uncles have this ability too. When I was living and working in London, I would come home and share experiences with my 'Grandpa'. His chair was at one side of the black range in the kitchen, with my grandmother's at the other. They would snarl insults at each other across a smoky fire, while their cat, RAF, slept on a square of blanket in the warming section of the oven, with the door open. My Grandpa kept his collection of pipes close to hand on a shelf above the oven. They were in a little wooden rack with tapers to light them at one side. He made his own tapers out of newspapers, spending hours carefully and precisely folding them. I loved it when he filled his pipe. 'Pass mi baccy, lass', he'd say. Then he would settle back and tell me about the times when the Round House in Chalk Farm was a shed for storing locomotives, and about the variety theatres he used to visit on his stopovers up and down the country. Whether he had had a private education or not, he had a thick Cumbrian accent. He would say to my grandmother, 'Ginny, put some watter in the kettle'. This rings in my ears even today.

My grandfather was very fastidious. For him everything had to be right. My grandmother put it down to him being 'brought up in a hotel' and it annoyed her. His table always had to be laid with absolute precision, correct knives and forks used at every occasion. He would wash all his hankies himself, and dry them in front of the fire, pulling out the creases. He was always spick and span. Grandpa used to buy his clothes off a Mr Brown of Bewsey Street, Warrington; in fact, as far as I can make out, he bought most things for the house from Mr Brown. Mr Brown sold everything: sheets and blankets, counterpanes, chenille curtains and tablecloths and, in particular, big wide curtains with scollops, which he bought for the sitting room. Grandpa used to pay Mr Brown five shillings a week, and when he bought a suit it would go up to ten shillings. He would come every Tuesday morning for his money and, as Auntie Ena recalled, 'He would sit jangling to my Dad about the old days. He had a cup of tea and sometimes my mother would do him a bit of bacon.' She went on: 'Christmas we always got new curtains and a new tablecloth. We used to look forward to this. My Dad had this purse – a little round purse. He would get it out and all us kids would say, "Oooooh, he's opening his purse!". And out would come your penny. Sometimes we would see my Dad was sucking something and he would give us a throat lozenge. He would snap them in two and we would all get half.'

'Just think', my mother recently reflected, 'didn't we think it was nice when he broke that bloody thing in two? In this day and age it would mean nothing.'

I never got lozenges from Grandpa, but I do remember, a generation later, getting pennies from the same purse. When he died, very suddenly, at eighty-eight, I was working in a show in London. When I came off stage the director told me the news. A light went out in my world.

From that moment, all that concerned me was that I should be present at his funeral. The theatre company was caring and allowed me leave. An actress friend lent me her best black dress and hat. I caught the train home. It was the first time our huge family had all congregated together at my grandmother's for some years. It was with little joy that they gathered there this day. Walking into that familiar kitchen and turning to look at the empty chair with his pipes and tapers still on the fireplace was too hard to bear. The hearse arrived and preparation for departure for the service began. I became aware that only the men were leaving.

'It's a private funeral,' my father explained kindly, 'there'll be no women.'

I felt an awful anger inside. I couldn't be denied this, it was my place to be there. I wanted to be there; needed to be. It was an intuitive need, desperate almost. As the men left I felt slightly ashamed, it was me – the messy one, the odd one out – causing a scene again. Once again I was not accepting the *status quo*. My Uncle Dave slipped back and handed me the keys to his car.

'If it means so much, then you go, love,' he said quietly.

I drove his pale blue Triumph Herald through the streets of Warrington behind the line of black cars. We stopped in procession as the traffic lights changed to red. Another sad family event crept into my mind. My Auntie Ena's first child had died just a few minutes after she was born. They had named her Maureen. Auntie Milly told me the story:

'When Ena's Maureen died, they said she needn't have a church burial because she had only had a little breathe. But Clyde said, "No, she's going to have a real little coffin". And his workmates made it. Clyde and I went to the cemetery to bury her, just us two. I had her on my knee all the way to the cemetery.'

At the crematorium I stood some distance away and watched the men take the coffin from the hearse. Six sons, six brothers: my six uncles carrying the weight on their shoulders. They were unexpected, the feelings this image provoked. It stays in my head even now, like an old photograph. Whether or not it was wise for me to be at the funeral I will never know, for it was very painful. But I believe we have to grieve, we have to cry. I did enough of that for all the other women at home putting the last touches to the ham tea.

When I lost my grandfather I lost a man who loved me, and who approved of me and my life without question.

My grandmother, from her seat at the other side of the fire, had always said that 'When he dies I'll bugger off. I'll go off and enjoy myself.' They'd had this relationship which to any outsider would have seemed like a matrimonial disaster. Mostly their arguments were over the fire, in both senses of the word. My Auntie Milly remembers:

'My father was a railway man, and he liked to do his own fire. He placed cobs of coal and all the slag around it. It was an art. And then as soon as me mother walked in, she'd go poking around.'

When he died she didn't want to do anything. She just sat at her side of the fire and faded away. She just lost the will to live.

She'd met him when she was in her early twenties. She was a dressmaker then and her parents had paid for her to be trained. My great-grandfather bought her her own sewing machine. She would carry it for miles to the houses where she did the sewing. She used to reminisce about how 'smashing' it was, when she was on her way home, and my Grandpa would be there at the 'turn', to carry her machine the rest of the way home for her. My grandmother was twenty-four and my grandfather a year older when they married and in 1909 she had her first child, a girl they named Ena. She then went on to produce thirteen more children, a total of seven boys and seven girls in all, although sadly she lost a boy and girl as babies. The other twelve thrived, and are still thriving. All the children had several names, all the girls romantic and elaborate ones: Georgina, Millicent Amelia, Margaret Jane, Barbara Mary, Jean, Jocelyn. Auntie Jean always said they ran out when they got to her. My father's family, in contrast, had very blunt northern names as my Grandma Wright, who died shortly before I was born, being a practical woman, always said it was a waste of time to give children these glamorous names, as 'folks only shortened them anyway'. Consequently, I had a family of aunts and uncles called Alec, Bert, Harry, May, Ada and my own father, Fred.

My mother's mother was huge and round, with a face that somehow reminded me of a toasted bun. Her hair was silver grey and pulled back in a French pleat. When she washed it it lay so long that she could sit on it. She was big and generous; you felt safe when she held you.

My grandmother's good opinion was very important to me. I remember her appearing on my doorstep an hour before I was due to be married, cloth in hand ready to wipe 'that black muck off your eyes'. I wouldn't mind, but I'd chosen to marry in a church opposite their house, so that they wouldn't have to travel far. She crossed Warrington to wipe off my eye make-up. When I finally arrived at the church, I was terrified that she would disapprove of how I looked, and as I walked up the aisle, my Grandma turned, and I heard her whisper, 'Oooh, she looks lovely!'. And my eyes filled with tears.

My grandmother loved her food with a passion and she hated housework with an equal passion. Both of these things I now realize I have inherited from her. She could cook and bake. She made everyone's Christmas cakes.

'She was country born', my Auntie Ena informed me, 'so she knew how to do it.' And at the mention of country another memory came flooding back to her:

'Pace eggs!', she cried. 'She would save her onion peelings. She would boil the eggs very hard, then she'd wrap the eggs and peelings in rags and string them and drop them in a pan of boiling water. They'd come out all orange and golden.' Apparently if you were living in Cumberland, on Good Friday morning or Easter Sunday you would go round to your neighbours and give them pace eggs. Auntie Ena continued: 'They had ledges on the old-fashioned windows, the "throw ups", and on those ledges, if you went round Seton village, or any village in Cumberland, they'd be full of pace eggs. They still do it, but they take chocolate eggs now.'

It seemed Grandma could do anything, knitting and haircutting included. Anything that is as long as she didn't have to do a dish or scrub a floor. And as Grandpa was fastidious, she was the opposite. She would walk through the house ignoring the row of hooks in the hall, throwing her coat in the dining room as she passed. As her daughters berated her, and pointed at the hooks, she'd just say, 'Oh shush', and the coat would remain draped across the divan until somebody else tidied it away. The daughters would 'do' her bedroom. They would clean it and put everything away, and then put clean covers on things and make it all look lovely. Perhaps *I* should have had a small army of daughters!

Then there was her love of food. My Auntie Milly always said:

'I've gone in to visit when they were in their eighties, and they've been sat in the kitchen having their breakfast, and there's been bacon, eggs, sausages, a full meal. We used to say: "My mother has one meal a day – and it's all day".'

She was undaunted by fears of overdosing on cholesterol, and unperturbed about her size; her hair shone and in her eighties her face had hardly a wrinkle, despite the fact that she loved butter, and would slap it generously over everything she and Grandpa ate. When she was in her late eighties, shortly after the death of my grandfather, she had not been very well, and the doctor put her on a diet. She loved her food, and particularly, which we've all inherited, she loved her dinner. My mother said, 'Your Gran's been put on a diet'. But when we arrived to visit her one Saturday lunch time, she was sat on her own at the kitchen table in the window, eating from a plate loaded with mounds of potatoes, chops, butter, gravy, veg., the lot. My mother admonished her, 'Mother, you're supposed to be on a diet!', and in reply, she explained, 'I know, I'm not having any pudding'. That was the diet.

Auntie Ena, being the eldest, never worked. Instead she took over the running of the large family. This freed my grandmother, alongside producing children, to get on with her dressmaking. Her excuse for not doing the housework, as if she needed one, was to keep her hands decent for sewing wedding dresses. These dresses would mostly be made out of georgette – a delicate, almost sticky material that would easily cling to you. And she maintained that if she had any hard skin on her fingers she would not be able to sew it. She would sit in her front room, sewing from morning till night. Her meals would be taken into her. She wouldn't wash a dish, they would be there until the next day. You couldn't move in her front room for pins, cottons, rubbish and dishes on the floor. Auntie Milly had brought boxes home from the factory where she worked for all these bits of rubbish. But Grandma never put them in there.

'Ooooh, Mother!', Auntie Milly would shout, 'you do rile me. If you'd just drop your bits in there, we wouldn't have to keep cleaning up this room.'

'Oh, I've no time to think about that', was the only reply she'd receive. But despite this my Auntie Milly maintains:

'My mother, and I'm not bragging one inch, was a marvellous woman.'

As well as the business side of her dressmaking, she had six very attractive daughters to dress plus, it seems, all their friends. She would design all their clothes, poring over pictures in papers and magazines to make sure her daughters had the most up-to-date dresses, coats, suits and hats. She even made blazers and kilts, and if she found a doll she would dress that too. My mother remembers:

'She was girl mad, my mother. She wasn't against boys, but she was more for the girls; she could dress them.'

My Mum and Auntie Milly would go ballroom dancing; in fact my Mum at one stage was champion of Warrington. Grandma loved them to look different. Everyone would wait to see what the two sisters would be wearing. When they'd been younger, it was fancy dress. It seemed the whole of Warrington marvelled at her inventiveness. My mother recalls going as a fan, and on another occasion a hat box, while Auntie Barbara was Cupid. But Auntie Milly took first prize for The Three Arts.

When they were all dressed in these flamboyant costumes, they'd set off with the neighbours' kids all together in a taxi paid for by my grandmother – two and six a time. She would stay in her room, sewing on. She'd be doing embroidery, tailoring suits, making Easter outfits from brown velvet, but be making nothing for herself, happy to wear her off-the-peg 'floral wraparound'. And Auntie Ena would stay behind and clear up the debris. When the little Georgina was two years old Grandma had been dressing her and chastising her for the child would not keep still, but kept dropping to her knees. As it turned out, this was not through naughtiness, but the first symptoms of poliomyelitis – infantile paralysis as it was then known. She was left crippled in one foot. Nowadays, a small operation would have solved her disability. Her aunts, however, tried other methods. They were very strong Catholics and they decided to take her to Holywell in Wales to be cured. Auntie Ena tells the tale:

'When they sent for me, my Dad said, "She's not going". He didn't believe in it. So my mother, in a temper, said, "She *is* going". I can see the aunts now, on Chester station; I was about eight or nine. I didn't see them very often. They took me to the big hotel at Holywell. In the morning I got dressed in a white robe, and this is why I don't like water; there were two Sisters of Mercy in white. There's a bridge across to the big baths and people who could walk had left their crutches. To a child it was overpowering. I thought, "What are they going to do with me on this bridge?". They ducked me under the water every morning for a week. I was hysterical. That's why when I see water I panic.'

And my mother confirmed: 'She panicked when she saw water yesterday – it was only a stream.'

Auntie Ena finished: 'I wasn't cured, and they blamed me Dad because he didn't believe.'

But, like Cinderella, she married her prince, and when she did Grandma designed and made her beautiful satin wedding gown with embroidered beads, tiny pleats across the bodice and down the sleeves and a fashionable cowl collar.

The family collected together to buy Grandma and Grandpa a television. I have to emphasize that it was an extremely new commodity, which they had never seen before. A ritual evolved. At five-thirty every evening Grandma would head off to the bathroom, wash and brush her hair and change her clothes. Then she would return to the kitchen and, taking a straight-backed wooden chair, sit down in front of the television. 'Good evening,' said the newscaster. And 'Good evening', my grandmother would reply, simpering and cooing into the screen.

The only time I ever felt any hostility towards my grandmother was once when I was a little girl, and my mother had been taken ill. Grandma came to the house to care for her. Our house had only two bedrooms so we had to sleep in the same bed. I'll amend that: my Grandma was sleeping, and I lay cringing in the corner as this snoring monster tossed and turned across my territory. It was a very disturbing experience; suddenly she was Grandma no longer. I longed for the morning, when she would return to normal.

Every Saturday, most of the family would congregate at Grandma's. It was a time to catch up on each others' lives, and gossip. She would bake on a Wednesday and a Saturday, and her home would smell of apple, mince and egg custard pies, and her large cakes baked in the meat dish – all covering the kitchen table. And every Christmas, more or less the whole family would make its way back to the nest for celebrations. At Christmas we would all sit around the dining table. If our family excels at anything, then it's at throwing a party. They would all bring their own drink to add to the collection. Grandma would have a bottle of port wine and a bottle of sweet sherry 'in'. She never went any further than that. When I was small the water butt from outside the washhouse would be emptied and transformed into a bran tub. Everyone had to buy a present that mustn't cost more than half-a-crown. Then these were wrapped and put in the tub. In those days Auntie Ena and Uncle Clyde had a smallholding at the back of the house where they kept chickens, cockerels and ducks. When they killed a chicken the lads would get the feet; they would pull the sinews and make the claws move and chase the girls with them. One particular Christmas Uncle Clyde had one of these feet and he said, 'I've had a little thought'. He got loads of paper and made a big parcel, which he labelled 'To Mother'. They all called her mother, even her 'outlaws'. Auntie Ena laughed.

'None of us could stop it. We knew she was going to get this claw. Ooooh, but it *didn't* suit her! This claw came out – it *flew* out. We all screamed with hysterics. But she didn't think it was at all funny. And it spoiled our Christmas night.'

When I was very young Christmas Eves would be spent at either Auntie Milly's house, or Auntie Ena's, and we would congregate at Grandma's the following day for the big party. Slightly inebriated uncles dressed as Father Christmas, with giggling aunts to assist, would fill our pillow cases at the bottom of the double bed we three little girls would be pretending to sleep in. I remember once we desperately tried not to laugh at the antics of Uncle Charlie fumbling around in the dark trying to fill our stockings. As he left the room we crawled to the end of the bed to grope around, trying to work out what our presents were through the paper. One Christmas when we found chocolates, we gobbled the lot in one go, and Christmas morning found three violently ill little girls with no interest whatsoever in their new pot dolls.

Every year as I grew older, the size of this Christmas gathering would grow too. New boyfriends, girlfriends, husbands, wives and children all extended the family on and on and on. It was a terrible initiation for a new lover to arrive at a Christmas party. He or she would be swooped on and 'tortured' by attractive young aunts and uncles.

My youngest aunt, Jocelyn, had recently married John, a handsome young farmer from Chester. Marjorie, Pauline and I as young teenagers thought he

was the bee's knees. That particular Christmas my
mother's present to me had been a roll-on girdle, a pair
of seamed stockings and a pair of cream Cuban-heeled
shoes. I was to wear them to the Christmas party.
In these latter years we had taken to spending Christmas Eve at home, and travelling to Grandma's in the
back of my Uncle Ernie's big van. This 'uncle' was
actually my Dad's friend, and in the week he used
his van for delivering, door to door, his sales of hypo
and disinfectant. Needless to say, the van smelled
very clean.

It was into the back of this van that Christmas
morning that I self-consciously climbed with my new
grown-up legs. I was flushed with the exertion of trying
to trap the stocking top into the suspender, and as I
squashed down in the van, I heard one ping; I blushed
again, turning an even deeper red than I already was. I
longed for my socks which I had stuffed into the bottom
of my bag with my black flatties, just in case. My legs
were painfully thin and with those seams, one wobbling
up the back and the other making detours round the
calves, and unspeakably clumsy cream shoes, from the
back I looked for all the world like one of the chickens
that ran around at Uncle Clyde's.

It was thus attired that I entered the extremely
packed room at Grandma's. There was Uncle John; he
smiled and I responded. And then as I removed my coat
his eyes caught sight of my legs, and he threw back his
head and laughed.

I died.

I stood in the middle of that room and died. Then with
my eyes scalding, I rushed out and up to the bathroom
where I kicked off Cuban heels, ripped off the hated
stockings and struggled out of the incarcerating rubber

girdle, replacing them all with my comforting socks and shoes.

I never wore a girdle again.

'You'll never have a flat stomach', my mother would warn. But I didn't care. Eventually I came to terms with stockings and suspenders, but was still relieved when tights were invented.

Uncle John has always maintained that it wasn't my appearance he was laughing at; he said it was '. . . just the thought of our "Tomboy Sue" in stockings and heels'. I'm sure that's true, but for me it was a realization of my worst fears: that I looked an utter prat. Which I did.

Talking of tights reminds me of my Uncle Robert. For some reason he always ended up wearing them at Christmas parties, or weddings, or really whenever he had the chance. They were usually Auntie Milly's. He would dance around with anyone he could find. This was a problem for him because he was the worst dancer in the family. His legs were so thin, they put me in mind of an ostrich, they were even worse than mine. Why he wanted to expose them was a complete mystery to me. But he did. One Christmas he sat on the big step in Grandma's kitchen smiling benignly into a glass of vinegar. My other uncles had replaced the contents of his glass with this, expecting him to notice the difference. Whether he did or not we don't know, for he downed the lot and carried on dancing.

I hasten to add that for the rest of the year my family led sober and decent lives, but at Christmas, weddings and birthdays, we certainly knew how to let our hair down. I have felt loved and supported by all of them. A little thing Auntie Ena once said seems to sum the family up.

'If anyone was ill, all the family shed tears; it was like shedding into a pool.'

Of course I haven't yet mentioned my father's family: the calmer influence.

Just a few hundred yards from where I lived for twenty-one years was the home where my father lived for twenty-six years. Still living there as I grew up were my Grandpa Wright, my Uncle Harry and my Auntie May, while two doors away were Auntie Rene, Uncle Alec and cousin Alec. Other aunts and uncles and cousins were also in close proximity, so again I was lovingly surrounded by a host of relatives.

My Auntie May was my bolt hole, where I would run if I was in trouble, or needed advice, or help, or a home for the latest 'stray' animal that I'd collected. Auntie May would help out and take in the strays, and then be lumbered with them for years. She too, like my Grandma Cowan, was handy with the needle. She didn't sew for a living, in fact she was a midwife, but she did it for pleasure, and I am happy to say that doing it for *my* pleasure was one of her pursuits. My Dad's mother had died shortly before I was born. I always felt as if I'd missed meeting someone very important. My Dad always told me with great pride how she had at the end of her years at the convent school in St Helens been kept on by the nuns as a teacher without training. She was apparently a lovely woman and one to whom the whole neighbourhood turned with the trials and tribulations of their lives.

My godmother and cousin, Lavinia, was one of the most important influences in my life. It was through her that I developed a love of theatre and books. Every birthday she would take me to Liverpool, and we would have our 'dinner' – I believe it's called 'lunch' nowadays

– in Lewis's store in Renshaw Street. Always we would have this dinner, usually roast chicken as I remember, in the restaurant on the top floor, not going into 'self-service' and this gave the day a sense of occasion. 'Dinner' was six old shillings (thirty pence). Then we would go to the theatre.

It was usual for us to go to the Playhouse Theatre, unless of course there was a ballet at the Empire, and that would take precedence. I grew up on a diet of *Coppelia*, *Sleeping Beauty*, all kinds of Shakespeare, and a production of *Luther*. This was a bit advanced for me at the time. All I remember is watching in fascination as the leading actor spat volumes of liquid all over his colleagues and, indeed, over the first few rows in the stalls, whenever his soliloquies brought him down stage in front of the audience. Revolting as this experience was, it never put me off; and those birthday trips with Lavinia, I believe, sowed the seeds of putting myself at risk to work with spitting thespians.

2

Coronation and the street

STREET PARTIES were something we seemed to do a lot of in my youth; indeed, there was always a lot more communal activity in the street in those days. Rounders was a game that was made to be played in the road with gates and lamp posts as bases and an endless expanse to hit the ball into. You had to be a little careful, of course, for some neighbours didn't take too kindly to having balls thwacked into their prize snapdragons, and cries of 'Can we have our ball back, please?' would often be greeted with 'No! Get lost!'

I suppose it was easier to play 'out there' then, with very little traffic about. In the early fifties hardly anyone in our road had a car, and when we got ours, I think we were among the first. I remember it caused quite a stir.

First of all my Dad, with the help of Uncle Ernie, built a garage. This in itself caused great interest amongst the neighbours. Curtains constantly twitched as the structure took shape, and by the time our little front gate had been replaced by a double one, and a concrete drive laid down, my mother was being inundated with magazines from 'well wishers' – all anxious to know when the new car was arriving.

My father, not realizing how much interest this whole venture would give rise to, was getting increasingly embarrassed. And as the day of delivery drew near, he began making secret plans with Uncle Ernie, plans deliberately made to divert attention. Seven o'clock one Sunday morning found my mother and me peering anxiously up the road from her bedroom window. Suddenly Uncle Ernie's hypo van rounded the top corner and being dragged behind on a very thick rope was a large chunk of black metal. As it drew closer it did look a little bit more like a car – at least one wing and half the bonnet did. Rushing downstairs, we opened the gates and the doors of the garage and we all pushed 'our car' inside and out of sight.

Fortunately for us the one good wing presented itself at the only window in the garage, so my mother and I polished it until it shone and anyone catching sight of it through that window couldn't fail to be highly impressed.

There followed weeks of intensive work, and eventually it was brought out from under wraps, and our Morris Ten was driven forth by one proud parent. By then the whole of our avenue seemed to be in possession of Morris Minors, which were rolled on to drives on a Sunday morning for the trip to church, then polished and put away for another week. Ours, I am glad to say, was in constant use, even on one occasion by my mother, who on a trip to Ainsdale beach, famed for its long stretch of sand, mud, oil and, somewhere in the distance, the Mersey, took to the wheel and headed off for the sea at forty miles an hour in first gear. As the car hit the mud, it stopped and for a few seconds nothing happened; then, alighting from the car and with as much dignity as she was able, in high-heeled shoes, she left the beach, and never attempted to drive again.

That same year was Coronation year, and innumerable street parties were planned. Ours was removed from the street to a nearby school, which was much better, for we had the whole field to run our races on, and tea with all those jellies could be laid out in the hall in case it rained. As it was such a historic occasion we had an enormous amount of red, white and blue streamers, with flags of course. And at the end of the day, every child – winner or loser – was presented with a Coronation mug.

There was a real 'show off' boy who lived in our road. His name was Nigel, and his father was a policeman – he's probably a chief constable now – so if you're reading this, Nigel, nothing personal. He always had everything before everyone else. Anything you had, he'd already had it months and got six of them; you know the sort.

One day, it was still 1953 and we were eight – I remember this very particularly because it was Coronation year, and that's a salient point in this story – Nigel arrived at school to announce to all that his family was in proud possession of a television set. He grinned and gloated, and everyone seethed. Television sets were still a rarity in working-class houses at that time. This went on for days; every morning we would be greeted with descriptions of programmes which we were regularly missing. And we, feeling our lives becoming drabber, and Uncle Mac on the wireless becoming less attractive, pretended not to listen, not to be affected, while secretly longing to see the apparently incredible, mysterious Muffin the Mule.

One morning, after one of Nigel's now famous TV critiques, I could bear it no longer, and suddenly out of my mouth shot the immortal words:

'Well, we've got a tele now.' There was a tremendous silence. Every eye was on me.

'Liar!', exclaimed Nigel – correctly.

'No I'm not, it's coming this morning', I retorted, wondering who was in control of my tongue. I stood my ground, knees braced, praying that I wouldn't go red or start shifting about.

Nigel stared at me long and hard. I knew he didn't believe me. I could tell the others were flummoxed, half wanting to believe, but very doubtful. The teacher arrived, and the debate halted.

At lunch time we clattered into the playground, and I knew the questions would come thick and fast. There was no way out now; I was caught in a lie and felt dreadful, but I clung on in desperation. Nigel went home for his dinner. We were all back in the classroom when he returned. He approached me and held out his hand.

'I'm sorry', he said sheepishly, 'I'm sorry I called you a liar.'

And with that he went to his desk, took his books out and afternoon class commenced.

I was totally mystified. And not only mystified, but bewildered too. I fretted all through the lessons. What game was this he was playing? What trap was he setting for me? At the end of school I walked home apprehensively, expecting a bombshell at every corner. I was racked with guilt; my Dad had always said, 'Be sure, your sins will find you out'. As I turned into our avenue, I glanced nervously at the house, then stopped in complete amazement. There, perched on our rooftop, was a huge television aerial. A great letter H signalling the arrival of a television set into the Wright household. With mouth still wide open, I ran into the house. Gathered round a little brown wooden box with a screen nine inches wide was half the family, looking absorbedly at the blank screen, while my mother reorganized the furniture around it.

'Surprise!', everybody shouted.

Surprise? They would never know the inadequacy of that statement.

Fate had smiled on me that day. Why, I'll never know.

On Coronation Day, you could hardly move in our house, as friends and family gathered round the Bush television – for that was its make. I remember it being very pretty, but very small. The lights were always turned out to watch, and we were allowed only a small table lamp in one corner. It was very cosy. Later we bought a magnifying glass which enlarged the screen to twelve inches. The only drawback to this was that you had to sit directly in front of the screen, as the sides became so distorted. And later still there was colour television – a plastic strip of rainbow colours that you stuck on the screen. No one was very impressed.

I think my mother's opinion of television decreased after the highlights of the Coronation. One evening we were all watching a play and when a character shouted, 'He was running down the street with his arse hanging out of his trousers', quick as a flash my mother's hand was on the knob.

'We'll have no more of that sort of language in this house.'

Censorship had arrived.

3

How I won the war and other holidays

LIFE, OF COURSE, did not revolve only around school and television. There were the summer holidays. Those endless days you had to fill before you returned to school. There was the constant search for 'something to do'. At Auntie Ena's on one unimaginative day, Marjorie, Pauline and I were kicking our heels. Uncle Clyde was in charge of us this day, and it was to him we turned eventually for inspiration. He, however, was fully occupied in front of the television. A cricket fanatic, he was determined that nothing short of an earthquake would draw his attention away from England v Australia in the test series of 1953, which was Len Hutton's last captaincy; especially not three little girls. But children who are bored can make very sure that if they're not having a good time, no one else is going to. Out of desperation will often be born the most inspired thoughts. Uncle Clyde in *his* desperation was duly inspired. He told us of the importance of the test match, he told us how the whole country was watching, and praying that England would win the Ashes; how everyone travelling on the train running past the end of his garden would be 'desperate' to know the scores. So why didn't we write these up on our blackboard and hold the results up for them to see?

'Wow! What a good idea!'

Not only did the railway track run past the end of Auntie Ena's and Auntie Milly's gardens, but here, at Auntie Ena's end, there was a signal and, if the trains didn't actually stop there, they slowed down, which would give all the travellers ample reading time.

We spent our holiday at the bottom of the garden.

We would run in and out of the house, and Uncle Clyde would write the latest score on a piece of paper, which we would transfer to the blackboard. The engine drivers, firemen and guards, and a lot of the passengers travelling up and down the same route, all seemed pleased to get the scores. We began to be looked for, and waved at, and when finally we wrote on our board in large white letters

'ENGLAND HAVE WON THE ASHES'

waves became cheers, and we were treated to blasts of steam and hoots from the engines. And a sigh of relief from Uncle Clyde.

Holidays seemed to have featured very heavily in our family. Somehow, even during the war, when money must have been short, a family holiday was always considered to be a necessity; quite sensibly in my opinion. I have my own childhood memories of these holidays of course, but one story I've always loved is of a visit to Gronant, in north Wales, towards the end of the war. My Uncle Clyde was not on active service during the war, but on duty at home, driving the fire engines. So on this occasion he was able to take his wife, that's my Aunt Ena, their daughter Pauline, my Auntie Milly and her daughter Marjorie, my mother and myself on holiday. A man he knew had a holiday bungalow in this little seaside resort, which is quite close to Rhyl, and the foolhardy man let us rent it for a week.

The three sisters and Uncle Clyde were shocked when they arrived; the bungalow was huge and beautifully furnished with an Axminster carpet on the floor.

'Good God!', exclaimed poor Uncle Clyde, 'he thinks it's just grown-ups and we've got these three young kids.'

The first thing they did was to turn the Axminster carpet over. This was a precaution against my and my cousin Pauline's behaviour patterns. Apparently, I was a 'tiddler'; in translation that meant that I would wee everywhere, everywhere I shouldn't that is. And so was Pauline. I hasten to add that I was only approximately eighteen months old at the time.

The walls of this residence were papered, and I had another irritating habit: getting my tiny fingers in the joins of the paper and ripping it away. I still love stripping wallpaper to this day; it gives me an enormous feeling of satisfaction. I had just got started on the holiday home when I was spotted. The furniture was quickly moved round, and the 'hole' covered with a large clock. From then on I was under constant surveillance.

By the end of the week the list of damages was quite extensive, and armed with a list – a new 'jerry', new lamps, light bulbs, mirrors and glue – my aunts and my mother set off on the bus for Rhyl. Being the baby, I had to go too, and miss out on a day on the beach with Uncle Clyde and my two little cousins.

As soon as the bus set off a terrible smell invaded the upstairs area. It was me of course, filling my nappy. The three sisters were beside themselves; this was just the beginning of the day. My mother stripped me, and slapped the offending nappy under the seat. They all prayed that they wouldn't be on the same bus going home.

It was while they were shopping for the replacements that they heard a large commotion in the street. Rushing outside they were amazed to see young lads dashing everywhere with placards. People were shouting; excitement was in the air. The placards heralded:

'The war is over!'

The sisters boarded a 'clean' bus and headed back to camp.

In the distance they could see Uncle Clyde on the beach, and the two little girls holding hands. No one on the camp knew, so they were the first to bring the wonderful news. Uncle Clyde danced on the beach. I got the credit for ending the war.

Apparently it was me filling my nappy on the bus that brought the war to an end. So says my family anyway. Sorry to disillusion you, if you believed it was due to our heroic army. My Auntie Milly told me this story. She finished it by saying:

'Unless you've suffered a war, you don't realize what it's like. You suffer in every way. You wonder if people are going to get lost or killed. It actually went on for another twelve months after that. My Dave was in East Africa, he had shoes made of snakeskin.'

Suddenly I had a glimpse of the sadness and reality of war.

There's another little story I grew up with about an incident that took place during the war. My father had been home on leave, and as the time drew near for his departure, Auntie Ena and Auntie Milly had come to the house to keep my Mum company and be there to cheer her up after he had gone. Saying goodbye to loved ones is never pleasant; saying goodbye in wartime with uncertainties about your loved ones' future must have been traumatic. Heaven knows what thoughts were in my parents' heads that day as my mother, by this time heavily pregnant, closed the front door on my father. The three sisters stood waving to him from the living room window as he made his way up the road. He looked round for one last wave, then throwing his kit bag over his shoulder, turned his back on them – and went smack, head first into an iron lamp post. The sisters collapsed with laughter. And as my father re-entered the house, dragging his kit bag, head dripping with blood, he was greeted by the sight of his wife and two sisters-in-law falling over themselves in their haste to reach the bathroom.

I know it's said that the summers haven't really got

worse, and that those long hot idyllic summers we had in our youth were no better or worse than they are now, but I don't believe 'them'. I remember one holiday so well. I would have been about seven, and the wild flowers and the poppies we gathered in the fields aren't figments of my imagination, for I have photographs to prove it.

We spent that hot summer in Egremont, Cumbria, at Townend Farm. The memories are steeped in nostalgia. It was harvest home, picnics in the fields, fresh farm food; and the gigantic pre-tractor carthorses – Blossom and Biddy.

Blossom and Biddy were huge majestic creatures. Chestnut brown, with white flashes on their foreheads, they were indistinguishable in looks, but not in temperament. We soon learnt that Biddy's was not the back to climb on to. We were far more welcome on the placid and beautifully doe-eyed Blossom. Biddy was temperamental and frisky.

At the end of the harvest there was a party. My father and uncles had been trying all week, with no success, to persuade my mother and her sisters to have a ride on Blossom, and on this special night they got them to agree. Grown-ups rushed for cameras, as we children rushed for Blossom. It was only when we were in the stable that the idea occurred to us: we would switch Blossom and Biddy. Suppressing our giggles to a minimum, we led out our neurotic friend, and the sisters prepared to 'board'. There they were, three sisters being hauled on top of the giant, who miraculously stood quite timidly while the mounting took place. Eventually all three were aloft. Little box cameras in position, and three grinning 'cheeses' ready to be snapped.

It was then that she took off. Biddy reared high and set off at speed down the road. Laughter changed to screams, and it was only the superbly fast reaction of the farmer that prevented a total disaster. I won't describe our punishment, although needless to say we fought very hard with arguments of mistaken identity. But I do have a wonderful memory of the three 'girls' with mouths wide open in shock as they prepared for take-off. It was only years later that I learned that all three had been in such terror that they had unceremoniously, and in total unison, wet themselves, and consequently poor old Biddy.

Actually weak bladders do run in our family. I remember a good holiday was always judged by the number of pairs of knickers hanging on the line.

Indeed, I suffered from the same complaint myself when I was a child. But sadly it was never viewed with such hilarity. This incident, or rather the way in which it was dealt with, gave me a complex for years.

The event took place while I was in junior school. We had all been crowded round the class clown, listening to his jokes and giggling uncontrollably. Unfortunately for me I was perched on top of a desk. As usual a lot of laughter produced in me a total and immediate desire to rush to the toilet. Well, in reality, there was never any time to rush to the toilet, it just happened there and then – uncontrollably and utterly, utterly embarrassingly. And that's what happened that day.

I was sat in a pool on top of someone else's desk, and the horror of discovery was too shameful to contemplate. Almost immediately the teacher returned to the classroom and we all scarpered. My misdemeanour, I prayed, might by some miracle remain undiscovered. But no, the boy whose desk was awash, raised his hand:

'Miss', he wailed, 'somebody's done a wee on my desk.'

At that age I hadn't learned the expression 'if the ground could have opened . . .', but it still wouldn't have been enough for what I wanted to happen. I felt sick and so frightened of the humiliation I knew would be mine.

'All stand', directed the teacher. We did so.

'All turn.' And again we did as we were bid. Then it came.

'You, Susan Wright.' That was my name. 'Go and get a cloth and a bucket.' Burning red from forehead to toes, my eyes watering, and trying not to hear the giggles and hisses from the rest of my class, I staggered from the room and from the school and down the road; and home. I was heartbroken. I would never be able to face anyone again.

Quite rightly my parents were outraged and visits between teacher, parents, and Head ensued. It was I, though, who had to walk back through the classroom door and face the accusing, laughing eyes. And although after treatment I was cured, whenever any other poor unfortunate left a pool, it was I who had the finger pointed at me. A lot of people do suffer from incontinence; it's a subject people find hard to talk about, and if they are dealt with in such an insensitive way as I was when I was a child, it's little wonder they find it difficult to seek help. If I ever met that teacher now, I think I would smack her very hard for that humiliation and the complex it left me with. I was left feeling ashamed and rather dirty, a feeling that, sadly, I didn't leave behind with my childhood, which, as you read on, you will discover.

 4 *'Say mama can I go out tonight?'*

NO ONE EVER took me to one side and told me about sex. No one, I mean, who should have done. I remember walking home with my friend from junior school, and her solemnly announcing that she knew what the word for *it* was. And although we were totally alone, she whispered closely in my ear, 'It's *fork* and the Queen does it'. I was appalled. The thought of the Queen doing it was so degrading; even worse was the thought of my mother and father doing it. I sought comfort in the fact that I was an only child, so they had probably only had to do it once. For months we believed 'fork' was the correct adjective for describing this belittling act, and little girls would go rushing giggling from kitchens all over the northwest when asked to put the knives and forks on the table.

Life continued like this for some years, with conversations full of misunderstandings and uproarious laughter at jokes that made no sense. I remember coming home from church youth club and asking my father what a 'prick teaser' was. That was the end of my visits to the youth club. One that kept me baffled for years was: 'Are you coming? No, I'm just breathing heavily!' I was an extremely naive girl. Going to an all-girls' grammar school didn't help. In an effort not to appear green I still continued to pretend that I was more experienced than I really was. In fact my experience at this point was decidedly nil. Although, in actual fact, I lie – I had been kissed by six different boys, all at once behind the air raid shelters in the school yard when I was ten. That had left me feeling quite hot and flushed. At grammar school we had a system of numbers to describe how far 'you'd been', starting at number one with a straightforward peck, and leading up to number ten – all the way with no precautions. I leave it to your own imaginations as to what two to nine involved! We used to stare in fascination at two of the older girls in our class, one of whom had been to nine and the other who had been to ten, seven times. They were obviously in control of secrets that we were desperate to hear about. In order not to appear too gauche about my limited experience I would add a few numbers on, with an air of quiet nonchalance, giving an air of:

'It always rather leaves me cold – it's a bit over-estimated, this sex bit.'

I used to have the most appalling crushes on the most weird and wonderful people. But the moment the subject of my desires came within three feet I would become tongue tied and red. There is another opportunity lost. Funny really, nothing ever changes. And why oh why was it that, even from the tender age of eight, the boys I fancied fancied my friends, and the ones I didn't fancied me? It was with such desperation that I planned to sit next to a handsome young boy with very nice legs called Gerald in my class at junior school, only to be thwarted by the unwanted attentions of Harold with the National Health glasses and buck teeth who was in love with me because of my eyebrows. He would spend all day trying to kiss me, which was nauseating, and Gerald was lost to me for ever. However, I did have some kind of kudos: little boys in those days all had fantasies of growing up to be engine drivers, and of course my grandfather was not only an engine driver, but he drove the *Flying Scotsman*.

The first time I really fell in love and wept tears of longing was over a boy I met at the forbidden youth club when I was sixteen. I was going there when I was supposed to be having piano lessons. I eventually got caught – I saw my mother meet my piano teacher outside the shops one day and knew then that the game was up, and the half-crown a week that I had been pocketing for so long, would have to be repaid to an irate father. The reason for my truancy was Kenneth Frogesham, a year older than me, who emulated Gene Vincent, who happened to be a hero of mine. Kenneth had a green Italian suit with the tightest trousers I had ever set eyes on, which he wore with huge winkle picker shoes. We'd walk along, never hand in hand, because he needed his hands to comb his quiff – which he did with astonishing frequency, perhaps just to avoid holding hands with me. He would sing 'Say mama, can I go out tonight?'. And I drooled. He left me for another, younger and prettier. And pregnant.

The next boyfriend I had would take me to the wrestling at the Stadium in Liverpool every Friday night, then we'd spend the rest of the night wrestling in the back of his van on the way home. Nobody really inflamed my passions as much as Gerald had done until I walked into the Cavern and saw John Lennon on stage. I was just eighteen, fresh from school, and in my first job as a tax officer in the Liverpool tax office. The club was round the corner, and the girls from the office used to be members. They took me with them during the lunch hours and it changed my life. I'd always loved music. Eddie Cochran had been another hero; I'd seen him on stage at the Liverpool Empire with the renowned Gene Vincent, and shortly after that Eddie was killed. I was in mourning for months.

There wasn't another place in the world like the Cavern Club, certainly not in my experience. Although I have to admit that at that point in my life my experience was restricted to St Helens Co-op Hall and Prescot Parish Church Hall, neither of which would find their names in the *Who's Who* of dancing venues. The first thing you noticed about the Cavern was the smell. It was so dark that you took in the odour while your eyes adjusted to the light, or lack of it. It was a dour smell that ate into your clothes, a mixture of sweat and damp, and the same mixture clung to the walls, giving the whole place a slimy texture. When you climbed down the stairs into the *bowels*, if you turned left past the bouncers – yes, we had bouncers in those days – there was a little snack bar where you could buy tea and coffee served in thick white mug cups and saucers reminiscent of British Railways cafés of the fifties. If you can't remember, watch out for the next repeat of *Brief Encounter* and you'll know exactly what I mean. I knocked a cup of this coffee over Ringo Starr on one occasion – the coffee was Camp, but Ringo certainly wasn't. The only food I can remember them serving was hot dogs, though I suspect there were probably cheese and ham rolls as well. Culinary bliss.

At the opposite corner to the snack bar, at the back, were the toilets. I mention this only from the point of view that the first and only time in my life that I've ever seen a rat was in those toilets. Such was my love of the place that it would have taken more than a few rats to deter me.

At this end of the club there was a hole in the wall called the cloakroom where sometimes you'd find a lass called Cilla Black, who worked there part time. Every so often – usually by a group called the Big Three – she'd be summoned to do a number on stage. If you chose that time to leave you'd have to wait until she finished banging it out before your coat was returned to you, often too late for the last bus. If we ever missed our last bus, which happened with increasing frequency, we'd get a network of buses going roughly in the right direction, then for the last mile or so I'd remove my stilettos and leg it like hell, hoping to get home before my Dad put the bolt on the door. If that had happened I knew I would be 'in for it'. My mother would take a sniff at my coat and announce to the street or whoever was interested that 'she's been wasting her life in that stinking Cavern again!'. I once tried leaving my night clothes in the greenhouse, and then climbing over the kitchen extension with the intention of climbing up the drainpipe to the sanctuary of my bedroom. I had, however, forgotten one vital ingredient in this cleverly devised plan – to leave the window open. As I clattered down the roof again I was greeted on the ground by a stony faced Dad. I didn't see the Cavern again for a month. History repeats itself. Only recently my mother confessed to me that she used to get up to similar tricks, and would meet the wrath of her own father. She told me:

'We used to sneak out to meet these lads and one night my Dad guessed where we were going. He didn't like you going with boys, and he's hit me many a time. Sometimes he used to embarrass me in front of them all.

I stood there wishing he was dead. I would leave my dance shoes on a shelf in the outside lavatory, so that he wouldn't know. I went in the toilet one night and this strange man was there, drunk with a cap on. I ran into the house screaming my head off. My Dad went out to find him, but he had gone. What he did find were my shoes.' She went on, 'And my mother was as bad; she'd be in the front room sewing, and watching out for us coming home. You could see the curtains twitching. I'd have to get off your Dad's motor bike higher up the road. But she was never fooled. When I got in, she'd give me a clip round the ear, "Stay off that bike", she'd say, "and another thing, you're not going with no lad from Liverpool".' But that wasn't the end of my mother's forays.

Nor was it the end of mine; my visits to the Cavern continued. I still think it was the most exciting place I have ever known. We went through a phase of dressing from head to toe in black. Black ski pants or black drainpipe trousers you were poured into. These were worn with huge black mohair sweaters over black polo neck jumpers. It all added to the sweaty atmosphere. The Cavern had previously been a jazz club frequented by students, and it was they who had devised a dance called the Cavern stomp – a variation on the jive but more of an unenergetic hop and skip, with your legs moving in one direction and moving your partner's arm violently in the other. The dance sort of evolved out of necessity: the lack of space, the incredible heat, the number of people and the amount of clothes meant that there wasn't the room to do anything more exacting.

Running down the centre of the Cavern, underneath the arches, were rows of little wooden chairs facing the stage. I use 'stage' in its most flattering form. All dancing took place at one side of the club but, as the groups got more and more popular, the dancing became less and the watching more, with people pressing and leaning over each other at the sides, desperate for a view of their favourites. Sometimes they even slept out all night to get a good seat at the front. I never did indulge in that activity but, when the Beatles were at the height of their popularity, I understood it completely.

In those early days of the Cavern, the Swinging Blue Jeans were one of the major groups in the city. Their music was a mixture of jazz and skiffle, although they might not thank me for that description. It was only later, as the popularity of the Liverpool sound grew, that they developed a different style. But they were always great, always entertaining and hugely popular. They used to have a spot at the Cavern called Blue Jeans Guest Nights, and it was on one of these guest nights that I first saw Gerry and the Pacemakers. I loved Gerry, with his huge cheeky grin and his twinkly eyes. I loved his music too; my favourite was a song called 'Pretend', an old Elvis Presley number. I always besieged him with requests to sing it. There were so many groups: the Searchers, the Big Three, the Merseybeats, to name but a few, and the Manchester invasion of Freddie and the Dreamers and the Dakotas. But above and beyond all these groups there were the Beatles.

I think from the beginning I always knew that the Beatles were something special. I think everyone who saw them in those early days knew this. They had those magical ingredients of charisma and magnetism. They could do anything, say anything, play anything. And we all ate obligingly out of their hands. Their impromptu rendering of 'Have a go Joe' with Paul on the piano was a particular favourite of mine. Lunch time sessions – a shilling to members and lasting two hours – would generally begin with Paul's version of 'Red sails in the sunset'. Nat King Cole would never have rendered it thus, but I bet he would have enjoyed it, nevertheless. They looked, to my mind at any rate, magnificent: tight black leather trousers, white T-shirts, short black leather jackets, generally unshaven – well at least Paul usually was; I think he had a problem with a five o'clock shadow. And of course, there were those famed mops of Beatle hair. They would emerge from the band room through a hole knocked in the brick wall – a short climb to the stage. The place would erupt. General banter between themselves and the crowd would occur, while a lightning tune-up would take place. It was usually Paul and John who were the protagonists in this repartee, and the Cavern resident DJ, Bob Wooller, was often the butt of their jokes. Whenever they played their rendition of 'Boys', instead of vocalising the usual chorus, 'Bop shua shua Bop shua', or words to that effect, they would often sing, 'Bob Wooller, shoot Bob Wooller'. Relations between John Lennon and Bob Wooller often seemed a little strained. I remember at Paul McCartney's twenty-first birthday party, a few of us were gathered in the hall when the front door was thrown open and the dramatic Lennon burst in and, leaning against the wall, he cried:

'I've just killed a man!' There flat out in the garden, was Bob Wooller, not dead, I hasten to add, just 'laid aside'.

When the Beatles sang it was Paul who brought the energy, but for me it was Lennon, legs apart, knees slightly bent, who brought the intensity and the sex.

There were no *poseurs* at the Cavern, indeed not from any of the groups in those days. All had a genuine love of playing the music, an enjoyment that was shared between themselves and their audience whom they would join later for coffee at the bar. Blissful days.

Pete Best was still the Beatles' drummer. Handsome and aloof, he always seemed to me to be the odd man out, a little bored with it all. It was no surprise when he disappeared, and we were introduced to Ringo, who was to be the new drummer. Stalwarts like myself had already seen Ringo play with a group called Rory and the Hurricanes. On one particular day that stays in my memory, John announced that they had 'learnt a new tune' – it was 'Twist and Shout'. We went wild. It was agonizing when they disappeared to Hamburg to play at the Star Club, although I still treasure a letter from Paul, telling me amongst other things about their long discussions about religion with Little Richard. My head reeled. They recorded 'Love me do' and Paul gave me a copy he had recorded on a little reel-to-reel tape. I kept it for years until it was stolen from my flat in London. Then there was their first television performance. They were on *Scene at Six-thirty*, a northern news programme introduced by Gay Burn. I loved them. My parents hated them.

'So they're the dirty Beetles who play at *that* place, and come to this house', my mother wailed. She turned to my father: 'I told you she'd come to no good roaming around Liverpool, Fred.' Indeed, on several occasions Paul *had* been to the house. I would proudly collect all his cigarette stubs after his departure to abate the insatiable demand of the girls in my road. 'Please please me' was released, and they began to travel further afield. Paul bought a new car, a green Ford Escort. We

ran out of petrol in it, outside the abattoir on Prescot
Road. The very last time I saw him I was hidden in the
back seat, under a pile of coats, while he and Ringo
drove past the Cavern. It was their return to Liverpool.
They were at the top of the hit parade with 'She loves
me'. They thought the fans might have deserted them,
as they felt guilty that they had deserted Liverpool. But
no, their fans loved them. And as proof they were
queuing outside the Cavern in their hundreds with
eighteen hours still to go before the concert began. It
was inevitable that we would lose them; they were too
special, their talent too great. They had to be shared
with the world. But I am glad that just for a few short
years they touched my life.

Funnily enough, I met my first serious boyfriend in
the Cavern. And of course he was a musician. But then
every other male in Liverpool seemed to be a musician
in those days. He was a few years older than me and, in
my eyes, extremely handsome. He wasn't a full-time
musician, more sort of semi-professional. In the early
days of our relationship, he was a motor mechanic,
working in the garage by day and playing in the clubs by
night. He had a little green Morris Minor van and we
used to pile the equipment into the back and set off to
the clubs. I was in an elevated position now: I was 'with
the band'.

I once took a week off work to join them on tour with
the Rolling Stones. We in the north had always seen the
Stones as the south's opposition to the Beatles, and
later there was a saying:

'While the Beatles were singing "I want to hold your
hand", the Stones were singing "Let's spend the night
together".' The general opinion among parents in that
period was that the Stones were dangerous, and the

Beatles were safe. All I know is that they were two groups who brought about a radical and exciting change to British music at that time.

As my boyfriend's group gained in popularity, he was away from home more and more. He would return to Liverpool dressed in his trendy gear. One day he arrived in a roll-collared shirt – navy blue with white polka dots. I thought he looked divine, but my Uncle Gordon was visiting at the time.

'You look like a big Jessy!', he proclaimed with disapproval. Whatever my uncle thought of his taste in clothes, I *loved* him; and he brought a whole new world to my door.

I was brought up in a rented terraced house on the outskirts of Liverpool – in Woolly-back Land as the 'scousers' call it. From being able to walk, I think, I used to take the same route – to school, to church, and to my friends' houses. Past Harry Preston's who I always believed pinched my tortoise (I thought it was mine because it had a white spot on its back), over the railway bridge, down the hill and into the housing estate where my friends lived. A large detached bungalow had been built on this hill and coming from a rather small house I found this building very impressive. One day on one of my sallies to my friends a little black car pulled up in the drive and out of it jumped the most handsome man I'd ever seen.

I think I must have been about fifteen at the time, and he must have been at least twenty-one. He was blond, slim and, on the occasion of that first glimpse, dressed in an elegant grey suit. I was captivated! The walks to my friends increased – in fact, we all started perambulating, arms linked, up and down the road, hoping for a glimpse of Mr Wonderful. No wonder I was so skinny in those days. Eventually we were on nodding terms. I think he would have been highly surprised if he had opened his front door and I hadn't been there. He must have thought I was part of the garden. One day, getting off the school bus, I spotted the now very familiar black car driving into the builders' yard. Was he visiting? Or could this be where he worked? Our walks changed location. And yes, this was his place of work. Although his being a builder didn't quite fit in with the image I'd created, I soon recompensed for this and wove a new fantasy around the new information.

Life continued in this vein for some time, nodding, blushing and giggling, until one day fate took a hand. My friend Jenny's parents had disappeared on their annual holiday, leaving their house 'available' for parties. During one of these epic events, Jenny was holding court, swinging up and down on a chair, in front of their vast plate glass window. Too much wine and an overemphatic statement affected her balance and the next minute she went arse over tit through the window. Amazingly, Jenny survived, which is more than can be said for the window. Always the one to turn a situation to my advantage, I saw my opening and took my chance.

'I know a builder', I said with great excitement; so did half my friends. We found the number and called the firm. I'm not sure how, but I think I must have discovered his name by this time, because we asked for him. And he came. The window was fixed up and so was I.

'Jenny, we've got to have another party.' So the next night, with the window back in place, and we having finished hand painting the frame with as many children's paint brushes as we could collect, and every bit of glass swept away, we had a party. And he came. Two days later he took me out on our first date. We went to the pictures in Warrington in his little black car. It seemed such a long way – it was all of eight miles. He was obviously a man who knew his way around. There was only one thing wrong with the whole deal: he was totally boring. I struggled on for at least a fortnight trying to endow him with an interesting personality, and then gave up. I then had to plan various routes to my friends, church and so on, that took me miles out of my way, or circuitous bus routes, anything to avoid the embarrassment of walking past the house. You might ask why I'm telling this story, and I think the reason is this. I have a terrible habit of embellishing men with qualities they don't necessarily possess – qualities which I want them to possess; qualities they can never really live up to. I have a history of this.

And what of my own life up to this point? I had left the tax office behind me with a breath of relief and had gone to work for Peter Brown at Nems – Brian and Clive Epstein's store in Whitechapel, Liverpool. Brian had become the Beatles' manager. He had dressed them up and given them an image; other groups followed. They would troop through the record store up to his offices above and sign requests for photographs until the demand became too great. Then we would go up and use the little roller which magically reproduced their names. Their increasing popularity meant increasing hard work for us. And by the time 'With the Beatles' was produced, we were working through the night to keep the shelves stocked. My own friendship with the Swinging Blue Jeans had developed, they borrowed my copy of Shan Romero's 'Hippy hippy shake' and recorded their cover version that went to number one. Later they borrowed and covered my copy of Betty Everett singing 'You're no good'. It became another number one. I demonstrated the latest dance craze – the shake – on stage at the Mardi Gras, Liverpool, with my friend Olwen, and our pictures were in the *New Musical Express*. When they appeared on *Top of the Pops* we were in the audience, dancing. At Paul McCartney's twenty-first birthday, I met the Shadows. Heady? I'll say. And I thought it would last for ever!

Suddenly I seemed to catch up with myself. The Beatles, Nems Enterprises and Peter Brown had gone to London. My first long-standing relationship had ended. With all the excitement of the last few years taken away I took a long hard look at myself. I had been living on the edge of other people's success. What about me? What was I going to do now – with the rest of my life?

5 *How to be a stick insect and stay sane*

WHERE DID IT all start, this desperate need to be slim, this agonizing battle over weight? Maybe I wished it on myself. I remember as a stick insect child and teenager desperately wanting to put weight on – to look like my Auntie Milly. Auntie Milly to my young eyes epitomised the womanly shape: rounded, warm and comforting. So what happened in those intervening years to make me, when I eventually reached the desired shape, react against it?

I remember the time everything changed. It was when I left home at twenty-two and went to live in London. I was only thinking the other day about why I love London so much. It certainly isn't anything to do with the traffic or tubes or the price of houses. It's where I made my first home, away from parental control. When I arrived in London as a young drama student my parents came with me. They were anxious to see their daughter settled in decent accommodation. We were all very naive, and were very shocked at the price of renting even a small room in Earls Court. My mother, though, was greatly relieved when she discovered the existence of an all girls hostel in that very area, so we went off to 'view'.

The lady who met us at the door was quite friendly and invited us in. All except my father.

'Men', she informed us, 'are not allowed across the threshold.' My mother's face brightened considerably. And upstairs we marched to inspect the room.

The rooms were depressing. Squashed into each were as many beds as it was possible to fit. Here was a lady obviously determined to take advantage of the shortage of accommodation. The room that was to become mine was on the first floor. Pushing open the door, you manipulated your body round the wardrobe and, stepping over the bottom of the first single bed, covered with an orange candlewick bedspread, you were then able to stand in the centre, jostling for position with a small formica topped table and three upright chairs. There were only two other beds in this room; it seemed that the one by the door, the one with the orange candlewick, the one you had to step over, was to be mine. The other two were already occupied, one by a glamorous art student, on a below-the-poverty-line grant like myself, and the other by a young Australian woman 'doing the city'.

Outside the 'bedroom', in a recess on the landing, was the hallmark of London bedsit living: the Baby Belling. For sixpence in the meter you had the privilege of its use. The first time I used it was a lesson to me. My sixpence went in, my small pan containing water and egg went on, and I retired to my room for a few minutes to await my culinary delight. When I returned, my pan with its egg was pushed back off the Belling, and various other pans were fighting for space on the oblong shaped hot plate. When all were removed the meter ran out and my egg was raw. It was the same with the bathroom. Sixpence in the meter would allow you a few inches of hot water; the taps were tied up with tights. It's a perverse picture I have in my mind; I hated bathing there. Someone would pinch your water and you were left in the cold looking at those wet dangling tights. I loathed this place. When I left home my mother, upset, had said, 'My life has ended now', and looking round this place I rather thought mine had, I was so homesick. I had no money, my grant hadn't come through, everyone seemed so hostile and my great Antipodean neighbour returning from her follies late at night would always manage to step on one of my legs as she crossed my bed, making me scream out in pain. She would then proceed to stuff her face with all sorts of luxuries without offering me any, while giving a running commentary of the delights of her evening. It was such a desperate existence and one I hope never ever to have to repeat. Six weeks into my first term I began to make friends and a room in a flat in Notting Hill became available. Willingly and happily I accepted. My new flat mates, both male, came to the hostel to help me move. I let them in. There was a screech and, like a scene from *Psycho*, 'Madam' hurled herself down the stairs and threw the men out on to the street. I lugged my belongings down from the bedroom and across the hall myself. I shut the door and didn't look back. Poor woman. I don't believe she ran an all-girls' hostel for their own protection, but rather as some indictment of her own hatred of men. I wondered what had happened to her that she felt such animosity.

From then on everything changed and it changed for the better. My grant arrived, my debts were paid and my new room in the flat was 'home'. Suddenly I was free to spoil myself. At home condensed milk sandwiches, or conny-onny butties as we called them in Liverpool, were forbidden, custard pies were rationed and chocolates were a weekend treat. Now I could fill my fridge with tins of condensed milk, with custard pies and chocolate, on which I could relentlessly gorge myself. And I did. Through all of this I never once thought I would become fat; it was just a 'treat'. But of course eventually it happened. The endless thin/fat battle had begun.

In retrospect, I can see the pattern. When I am unhappy, lonely, bored or pre-menstrual, I seek solace in the same rich comforting foods as I did all those years ago when I was too naive to understand what was happening to me.

In those heady days of the sixties I was a young trendy drama student living in London, and living it to the full. With the arrival of the mini skirt came the arrival of the boiled egg and grapefruit diet. Who could be fat and wear a micro skirt? But life was active and weight seemed controllable again. The pattern was always the same: when life was full and exciting – weight no problem; with loneliness and depression – weight a *huge* problem. During one of my eating phases, still living in London and in despair, I took a visit to the local doctor. He was a dinky little man and kind; I felt embarrassed and rather weak – it seemed absurd not to be able to control your appetite. He appeared to understand. With the ease born of a doctor free to do so, he wrote me out a prescription for Dexedrine, little yellow slimming pills which I dutifully took. Pow! Everything changed. I totally lost interest in food. I drank black coffee by the gallon, smoked like a chimney, gabbled non-stop and cleaned the flat from top to bottom, and bottom to top again. The weight, as you can imagine, dropped off. This was it; end of problem. I was a stick insect again, and felt fantastic. Then the pills ran out. I trotted back for more, this time with instructions from my friends to get some for them as well. My dinky kind friend was extremely apologetic. He was afraid to say he couldn't give me any more. A black cloud descended. We talked for a while, the doctor and I, about the problems of putting on weight, and being an actress. I must have touched a chord somewhere; he told me to wait, left the room. I sat for a while gazing out of the window down on to the busy street below and to my surprise I saw him going into the chemist on the corner. A few minutes later he was back at his desk clutching a brown paper bag containing the precious pills. 'These will positively have to be the last', he said.

When I look back now, I am appalled. I am appalled at the doctor for behaving so irresponsibly, and I am appalled at myself, for being so much more concerned about the discontinuance of my easy 'slimming pills', than having consumed, even if in a small quantity, a dangerous drug. Although today these kinds of drugs are no longer prescribed for women wanting to lose weight, there are, however, on the market a lot of products tempting us to quick solutions that have unknown or possibly dangerous side effects. How much are we prepared to risk for the 'perfect shape'?

Life went on for me like this for years. With hindsight, I can see that the extremes in my life were enormous and so was my weight. I had a fat and a thin wardrobe. On a couple of occasions I even outgrew my fat wardrobe. Then I would hide from the world seeking solace in food. Always somehow I would find some sort of strength to drag myself out of the situation – back from the brink of despair. It was gradually dawning on me that it wasn't pills I needed; from somewhere I needed to get the willpower to get control of myself again. A friend of mine, back from America, had visited a hypnotherapist there, to help him give up smoking; it struck me that this was a similar problem. Maybe hypnotherapy could help me.

It was difficult to go about finding one; the only thing I had at my disposal was the Yellow Pages. But there the hypnotherapists were. And, believe it or not, listed under 'Hypnotherapist'. I thought I'd go for the woman; she would probably be more understanding. It took me ages to find her offices. I had this irrational feeling that I was doing something rather distasteful and the fact that the offices were in a back street and up endless back stairs did nothing to alleviate that feeling. By the time I arrived at the door, I was in a panic. The waiting room was tiny with two little wooden chairs pressed tightly together and a few tatty magazines scattered on the floor. A woman was sitting on one of the chairs. I sat down close to her; we nodded at each other sheepishly and then tried to pretend we didn't exist. The room was only separated from the 'consulting room' by a thin partition. Through this thin partition I could hear every word of the consultation. A man, presumably deep in a trance, was being warned of the horrors of smoking. He was told he would never want another cigarette, and if he ever lit one, he would be violently sick. It was rather embarrassing sitting there, eavesdropping on this life and death struggle going on in the other room. I knew then if anyone came in to the waiting room after me, I would do a bunk. A few minutes later the ex-smoker came through the door. We all nodded again, still sheepishly. Suddenly his hands went to his pockets, and a fag was in his mouth. His wife made a grab.

'What are you doing?', she screamed. As he ran out, I could hear him down the corridor saying:

Grandma and Grandpa, The Duke, Cowan with the
dog, Mac.

Topless beginnings. l to r: Susan, Pauline, Marjorie.

Grandma's skating
dresses which we never
skated in. l to r: Susan,
Marjorie, Pauline circa
1948.

My 'Aspiration': Auntie
Milly.

'You're not going with no lad from Liverpool': my
Mum and Dad get married.

Cinderella with her prince: Uncle Clyde and Auntie Ena.

Uncle Robert. Proving that there is more to him than just a pair of legs.

'. . . We will fight them on the beaches.' The girl who won the War.

Dad – home on leave.

Post-war holidays. Me and
my Mum on the front at
Scarborough, 1948.

Susan and Marjorie, heads
chopped – but yes, there
were wild flowers.

Three sisters, three husbands, three daughters. Top
row: Fred, Margaret, Dave, Milly, Clyde, Eva.
Bottom row: Susan, Marjorie, Pauline.

Back in Gronant again. l to r: top row: Auntie Milly,
Grandma, Auntie Ena and Mum, l to r: bottom row:
Marjorie, Pauline and Susan.

Susan, Marjorie and Pauline, London. Just look at
those legs; Uncle Robert eat your heart out.

'I just want to see if I'm going to be sick.'

'Now Johnston', I said to myself, 'are you serious about this?' Before I could answer, 'Next' came a voice through the partition.

I felt about five years old. I crept in. The woman at the desk turned to greet me with a huge smile. Suddenly all my fears vanished – here was a woman I knew I could trust.

And I was right; she was amazing. She was hugely overweight, smoked like a trooper, wore a wig – I later learned that she had lost her hair through having chemotherapy treatment and that she had had a breast removed – and with all this and running a business, she was also bringing up a child on her own. I often wondered if we were sitting in the right chairs and if perhaps I should have been holding *her* hand. That's what she did – she held my hand. She listened. At first I could hardly speak, hardly bear to admit I had a weight problem. Slowly, very slowly all the anxieties of the last years began to trickle out.

I'm not sure if I ever 'went under'. I was always aware of the telephone ringing, or of one of her great rasping coughing attacks, or that someone might be listening to me as I had listened to the smoker, but without doubt, it helped me, and I think I know why.

Nowadays my weight problem is not so extreme. I love food and put on weight easily, so there is a constant struggle, but nothing like the horror stories of the past. I know my problems were linked to unhappiness and now I am so much happier with my life. And the reason my hypnotherapist helped me so much? I talked about it. I saw I had a problem and sought help. And if ever I had such a problem again, that is what I would do. Seek help, face up to it and talk about it.

I first started smoking when I was fifteen or sixteen; my mother will be shocked when she reads this! It was a Friday night at the church youth club. That youth club certainly has a lot to answer for. One of the boys persuaded a few of us girls to have a puff of his Woodbine tipped. I puffed, I fainted. I didn't smoke again for twelve months.

A lot of people seemed to smoke at school; terrible when you think about it, girls around sixteen and seventeen years of age puffing away in the toilets. Even the prefects, sent to trap us, would book our names then stay for a quick drag. I don't think there was ever a thought of what harm we were doing to our bodies. No one really knew in those days. Or, if they did, they certainly weren't telling. We knew it was wrong because we weren't allowed to smoke at home, or to be seen smoking anywhere. But I'm not sure if I knew the reason why. It was like drink, something grown-ups did, and that one day you'd be old enough to do yourself. That it affected your health was irrelevant.

For years I smoked in secret, in my bedroom and in my friends' bedrooms. We would conceal cigarette stumps in jewellery cases or old bottles of perfume – anything we could lay our hands on. This would lead to eventual discovery and punishment. We used to be able to buy five Woodbines in those little triangular paper bags from the sweet shop which until so recently we had more innocently bought our sherbet dips in. My father smoked heavily, but he used to admonish me, saying I would regret it and should stop now while I could still control it. The truth was though, that I enjoyed it. It made me feel, and I thought made me look, sophisticated. I was grown up and in control.

I think that's always the relationship I had with a

cigarette. Whenever I found myself in a difficult situation, the taking out of a cigarette gave me breathing time. There was an immediate bonding between smokers who passed round cigarettes, a ready made companionship that non-smokers did not share. As the years went on, I began to understand what my father had tried to tell me. I always imagined that I would be able to give it up at any point, at any time. But the first time I tried, I realized how difficult it was going to be.

In the early seventies I became aware of the dangers of smoking; I also began to see how much money I was spending on it. I'll stop I thought and did. After a week of no smoking I thought, 'Well, I've done that. The only one I really miss is the one after dinner, in the evening.' I'd heard that cigar smoking was less dangerous, so I worked it out in my head, doing a very good job of convincing myself that if I had one cigar after dinner – well actually it was a slim Panatella – then life would be fine. When I was smoking twenty slim Panatellas a day I realized I had a problem.

There followed ten years of battling. I'd find excuses for not giving up: weight was of course a major factor, because as I downed the cigarette packet I would pick up the sweet packet. Every time I gave up, a crisis would erupt and I would reach for a fag. For example, a first night would approach and the tension would be so great I would just have to have a ciggy to get me through it. Under any sort of pressure I would barely be able to live without a cigarette in my hand. I even reached a stage when the first four or five of the day would make me feel violently ill, but I knew that, if I staggered through them, by mid-afternoon I would be enjoying them again. I had a terrible cough and if ever I got a cold it would always become bronchitis. It was a severe situation and one I couldn't seem to fight my way out of. What seems strange was that I had gone through my pregnancy with hardly a puff. If I could do it then, why was I incapable of doing it now? Obviously the thought of the unborn child and the protection of it mattered more to me than my own needs. I started to brain wash myself with these thoughts. At this time I had given up a secure job in Theatre in Education to go freelance. With the amount of money I was spending on cigarettes, I could pay my mortgage. But the biggie for me was that if anything happened to me, my child would be left without its only parent. And yet, despite this, here I was taking the risk of that happening. I continued to push these thoughts into my head and after a while my subconscious, stimulated by one final orgy of smoking, clicked, like a computer that has been fed information, and said, 'That's it. No more.'

I had been working in a play in London, and we were to have an end of run party. The party took place in my friend's flat, where I had been sleeping on the sofa. It was a great success, the usual sort of thing: lots of drinking, lots of smoking. Finally, when all had left I climbed into my bed in the 'party room'. When I awoke the next morning, which as it happens was only two hours later, I could hardly breathe. I must have witnessed that sight of overladen ashtrays and half filled glasses of wine and scotch so many times before, and yet for some reason that morning, my senses were acutely aware of the filth of it all. I was disgusted. I have never touched a cigarette since. That was eight years, three months, forty-two minutes and five seconds ago.

I have never lost my wish to smoke. I now feel outside that 'group' of smokers, although the fact that it is such an anti-social habit these days does help a bit. But I'm still finding myself walking behind people when they are smoking, taking in the whole *nostalgia* of the smell. The smell, paradoxically, was something else that helped me not to smoke again. I noticed how it clung to smokers: their breath, their hair and their clothes. I must have smelled like that. Not a pleasant thought.

I know that not for one minute would I ever dare to smoke one cigarette, for I would then smoke twenty. Over the years I have recognized that I am an obsessional person. I can't cut down – I'm an all or nothing person. I either smoke a lot or I don't smoke at all; I either eat a lot or I don't eat at all. There is no middle way! Having learned this, I feel that it is one step in the direction of taking control of myself.

It's not easy to give up smoking. The truth is that it's as addictive as heroin but considered socially acceptable, and the sad truth is that more women are smoking than ever before. A higher proportion of men give up than women. Or could it be that when men in the family give up they get more support than a woman in the same situation? I know the weight problem is an enormous pressure on women not to give up. I once saw a woman interviewed about smoking on a television documentary called *The Ladykillers*. Her voice rasped and was obviously damaged by heavy smoking, but her weight was her prime consideration and she couldn't give up.

It would be dishonest if I said that my weight didn't increase when I gave up smoking. Whether that's to do with overeating, or something to do with my metabolism, I'm not really qualified to say. But I do know that eventually it all evens out. To be able to smell and taste, to lose your hacking cough and feelings of nausea, and the continual worry of the effect on your lungs is well worth a couple of extra pounds.

It's amazing when you start to own up to things, how many other people are experiencing the same problems, and there's such comfort in not feeling isolated.

I wish I was braver, I wish I could say, 'OK, so I'm fat, but I'm friendly, so what?'. I've a cupboard full of work-out tapes downstairs and I wish I could use even one of them regularly. I wish I could organize my time so that I could join in with 'Mad Lizzie' on TV AM, but there's school lunch to pack, school uniforms to iron, dogs to walk. Always tomorrow, I'll find time to jog, swim, work out, meditate. It always seems to be me that doesn't find time or energy for any of these, but I don't believe I am alone. I think I am caught up in a world full of pressures which dictates how we should be, how we should feel.

To go back to the cupboard full of tapes – I've always enjoyed exercise, but I began to realize that I really enjoy it most in the company of others. To begin with, as the pencil slim child and teenager, I burned off energy in play and grinding away lunch time and night time in the Cavern and various clubs of Liverpool. It wasn't until I went to drama school that I experienced organized exercise. For us of course it was exercise with a purpose: it is essential that actors be fit; it is also essential that they have physical control and move their bodies well. This is applicable to us all, not just actors, but it is a great advantage for an actor to be able to dance or at least be able to move with grace across a stage. It was with this in mind, I am sure, that we were subjected to ballet and fencing for two years. I loved the fighting side of fencing, though I'm sure I didn't do it with much grace.

I know for an absolute certainty that I never attained the grace of a ballerina. Our French 'Madame' used to regard me quizzically out of the corner of her eye as I lumbered dangerously across the studio, 'pliéing' or 'jeteing' or whatevering. I think she preferred to think I didn't exist, and by the end of the course she had convinced herself of this. I was probably her greatest failure.

It was only when I was told in a critical note from the principal, after what I had believed was a triumph in acting, that I moved across the stage like a 'farmer walking through a ploughed field' that I realized the importance of movement. Modern dance was more rewarding. You were allowed to be much more expressive; given greater freedom. This I suppose was because it was less disciplined than ballet, and I have never been very disciplined. We were, however, carefully choreographed to Albinoni, and somehow or other in that dance I was able to express grace and control. I still can't hear that piece of music without remembering us all together, moving in unison – it's a very warm feeling. I always want to do these movements whenever I hear the music, but the steps are long forgotten.

Our other movement classes were hard slog work-outs, and later I suppose I enjoyed the Jane Fonda work-outs because they were very similar to the sessions we did as students in those days. I thrived on these, once, that is, I had got over the embarrassment of parading before everyone in my new black tights and leotard. No stripey leotards with high cut legs then, just very plain ones and black tights. Mine had feet in, and I used to slither all over the wooden floor. When we stood with our legs apart I nearly did the splits before I learned how. I noticed some girls had no feet in their tights, so I cut mine off and had to appear the next day with lots of little ladders running all the way up my legs. There were no mats to lie on either, just the hard cold floor, and so many mirrors. At least if you can't see yourself you can imagine you look swanlike. I found it a work of art in itself trying to avoid 'facing reality' by catching a glimpse of myself. It was a horrible shock when I came face to face with myself, sweat dripping, neck bulging, bits bouncing – could that body really belong to me? Why do I look so uncool in work-out sessions? I'm exactly the same on the beach; I've never mastered that one either. I always look hot and sweaty, the sand sticks to me and my hair frizzes. Where do these languid girls pick up their secrets?

Those work-outs were a hard slog, there was no getting away from that, every muscle stretched, but the wonderful feeling of control that a well exercised and fit body gives you made it all worth while. With this knowledge I wonder why I can't get my act together to do it now. The only drawback, I have to say, to these group work-outs, came during an exercise for stomachs. As we lay on our backs with our legs in the air, and slowly scissored them to the floor, an orchestration of vaginal farts would hit the air. This was totally embarrassing.

It was really when I went into Theatre in Education that I took all this experience and started to work out again. This was probably to do with the way in which we worked, often involving a lot of mime and physical activity. I remember a particularly lively production of *Romeo and Juliet*, when I worked with the Cockpit TIE team in London. There I was playing Mercutio, swinging in from the flies on a rope to grab an unsuspecting Tybalt round the neck with my legs (you see what I mean about having to be fit). The only way you take on productions like these is to work out as a group every morning. There has to be a lot of trust in a company, both physically and mentally, and that group activity every morning helped to achieve this.

My next stop was the Belgrade TIE team in Coventry, where again every day would start with this group activity, and my experience was extended even further. We were doing a play called *Drink the Mercury* by David Holman, based on the pollution of Minamata Bay in Japan; it was a pretty grizzly account of how pollution at its worst can destroy. Close to a little Japanese village a factory had been built on the Bay, which dumped its waste mercury relentlessly into the waters. This seeped into the plants, the fish ate the plants, the birds ate the fish, the villagers and their animals ate the fish. Mercury poisoning, of course, attacks the brain, and the effect on the village was fast and devastating. I don't want to sound smug, but fifteen years ago we, and many other TIE teams, were trying to point out the horrors of pollution and the destruction of the rain forests. Apart from our *Rare Earth* programme, we once turned the entire Belgrade theatre into a huge imaginary boat that took 400 children on an adventure trip up the Amazon. The main purpose of the journey was to show the children the gradual destruction of the forests: how roads were being built, trees chopped down and whole communities decimated. Through this they learnt of the importance of the Amazon Basin to the world, and how these forests provided a large percentage of the world's oxygen. If we could see it then, why couldn't anyone else? And indeed during the early seventies while doing this work we were told we were scare-mongering. I wish Mrs Thatcher had seen the programmes; maybe she would have gone 'green' then instead of now.

This story of Minamata was part of a three-visit school programme for top junior children; it was our second visit, homing in on a specific incident. It is obviously a very distressing story, and in some way we wanted to remove it slightly so that emotionally they could sit back from it. We decided to do it in the style of the Japanese Noh theatre, that is with storytelling, mime and mask. We employed a mime artist to teach us the techniques; mime involves such delicate control, and such precise judgement that when you went through one of his work-outs you *knew* you had really worked out! But for the first time the work-outs suddenly became not just for fitness, they were a method of expression; I discovered how to use my body to communicate. It was exciting stuff.

When our mime artist departed, we carried on using the things he had taught us. A new girl joined the company, Judy Spiers, better known today for her television presentation work. Judy was great; she herself was keen on fitness and brought a whole new dimension to the morning group. She was extremely strict with us, put us through our vigorous routines, and made us laugh till we ached. I remember Maggie Steed, who was in the company at the time, thanking Judy because she had managed to lose a stone without even dieting. Judy understood the weight problem; she always put her own in those days down to the pill:

'I'd open the door and my tits would come in ten minutes later. I couldn't cope with it; I would feel "Whose body is this?".'

Of course I never thought of her as being fat at all; in fact after she left Coventry she made herself nearly anorexic. She says now:

'I'd been so low, a stone or two stone lighter than I am now. I'd hold my teddy bear up in the mirror, because I knew the size of that teddy-bear – the mirror is deceptive.' She goes on, 'I had a girlfriend who was fat, I couldn't get her to come out. I'd only just become her friend, and I'd say "Get Andrea to come out". I'd ring her up and she'd say she couldn't come out because she was too fat. I'd respond, "Oh, fine! Well I'd stay in if I were you, and get depressed. You'll have a much better evening. I wouldn't care if you stayed in for three weeks and got thin, but you'll still be fat when you come out eventually!"'

Really what Maggie had said about losing weight was the cruncher: working as a team we were fit, we were fulfilled. We were losing weight because of the energy we were giving out and not because of any pressure upon us to be thin. It is the same sort of pressure you feel as soon as you say you are on a diet. You suddenly crave all the things you are about to deny yourself. I wish I could manufacture in a bottle that feeling of fulfilment, to be taken three times a day, for the times when all I can seem to think about is what I am going to eat next, and do I really have to take these dogs for a walk? And there's a funny thing, talking of dogs; they are now saying that walking is one of the best exercises you can do – I only ever thought it was good for the dogs.

When I first started work at *Brookside* I wanted to continue to fulfil my passion for exercise. I would take my Jane Fonda tapes in and do a work-out during lunch hour in the Grants' living room amongst the cameras and the lights. More and more people started to come, and what with all the paraphernalia of the shoot, there wasn't enough space for the kicking and stretching of legs and it became too dangerous to continue. In the end, we had to admit defeat and abandon the sessions. This was very sad because so many of us would have enjoyed the regular activity. But six years on, space is even more cramped so I doubt if we will ever re-form.

Having said all this, I know I would be being unrealistic if I thought it was easy for us to feel fulfilment all the time. But still we have to face the fact that we want to be fit and we want to be healthy and that takes us right back to diet and exercise. I am beginning to think that dieting is bad for you; it's a healthy way of eating that you have to find.

All these problems are not simple; it is like every day is a new battle.

For example, why, oh why, do I always walk out of the hairdressers with my hair a totally different style from the one I had in mind? Once home, why do I weep buckets and long for the old style which only yesterday I had so detested? I don't understand how it happens – even in my most assertive mood when I feel I really have described shape, colour, and perm so well, I feel myself sinking slowly down in the chair, as I am cajoled and wooed out of my aspirations and persuaded that their ideas are so right for the shape of my face, my colour tone etc., etc., *ad infinitum*. Every other woman in the salon – and often these days, men as well – walk out wearing the hair I was intended to have, and I am left with this odd growth which bears no resemblance to anything I ever picked out of *Hair* magazine. Some of the worst moments of my life have taken place in that walk from salon to my transport home, with eyes cast down and praying no one will recognize me, then once home, brush out, lacquer out, tears out. I know I'm not alone; how many conversations have you overheard that go like this?

'Honestly, just a little off the ends, you'll never be able to tell the difference, no really there'll be nothing off the length.' I'd never been able to work that one out.

And I've got a new battle now. The wrinkles and sags of middle age. I think it's thoroughly depressing to grow old; I hate all the lines and the grey hairs. I hate most of all people talking in hushed voices about the menopause – the next mountain I will have to climb! I'm easy prey to the cosmetic market. As every cosmetic company promotes its latest age-reducing anti-wrinkle cream, my head goes into turmoil. I can't use them all, so how do I know which to buy? Which one should I believe? They are all telling me that they are the most effective. Judy Spiers told me she had just spent £120 on Christian Dior anti-wrinkle cream. She said, 'If you buy two items of their Resultant Rapid Anti-Wrinkle cream, you get a free sample. So I bought four and got two free samples!' Actually the truth is, the only thing that is going to be effective in the end is plastic surgery. Would I have plastic surgery? Yes, if I'm honest, I have to say I would. I would love to look in the mirror and see a young face again, see a clear jaw line, without the chin hanging beneath it. Whether I ever will is another question. I have been going to have my nose fixed since I was twenty and I still haven't managed to get round to it. What we are really talking about is not being satisfied with the way we look.

One of the things it's important to remember is that television puts between eight and ten pounds of weight on people. So what you are seeing isn't real. Judy Spiers and I talked about this at great length because it's very difficult to watch yourself growing older on the television every week.

'It's unreal, what you are seeing there is artificial, it's

like photographs – they *do* lie. One's face is moving the whole time, in photographs it's iced. I know that to look brilliant on television you have to be painfully thin.'

She told me, 'You don't look older than when I last saw you ten years ago; now on television when I've seen you, I thought you had aged and put on weight'. In an earlier conversation I had with Clare Short, she talked of a similar dilemma:

'We live in a society of images. Everyone's beautiful – they all have these fantastic homes and cars and possessions. It's in our heads. In some way we emulate it, even if we think we are rejecting it. We are absorbed in it, all the consuming things, wearing things, cutting our hair. All that stuff. And it does give an image of glamour and ease, and sex is wonderful, and we end up in love for ever and ever. Which is of course a great big lie, and life is much more difficult and painful.'

Our lives seem to be a series of 'if onlys'. If only my nose wasn't this shape; if only I was taller; smaller; fatter; thinner; blonder; darker; younger; older. Then everything would be all right. Clare Short emphasizes this:

'We all worry about our appearance. Is my body okay? What clothes shall I wear? What about my Mussolini chin? You need some people to make you feel good. Then these things don't matter. Women are starting to do this naturally for one another, talking together, giving confidence, then suddenly it doesn't matter what your clothes are, if you've got any make-up on, or if you've got a spot, or whatever it might be. If you have one of those conversations, you begin to feel good about yourself. You know that feeling: on the same day, you can feel ugly and wretched, and then you can feel like the most beautiful person on the planet. Children need love; so do adults. If people love us, we feel good about ourselves.'

I think, in the end, it's about not valuing yourself enough. We've just got to like ourselves more. How simple!

6 *Cutting the umbilical cord*

IT WAS A long road that led me into politics – not that I'm really *in* politics – because the road goes on, and with it comes confusion and doubt. Certainly the search to 'understand' opened up for me a whole new way of looking at the world in which I had unquestioningly lived. I can never remember politics being discussed at home or at least, if it was, I never found an interest in it. But I do remember at general election time, my parents would dress in their best clothes and go off to register their vote with great pride. So it was instilled within me that to vote was an extremely important thing. I also recall sitting with my friend Bah, in 1960 at the age of sixteen, dressed again in my black ski pants and mohair sweater, outside Blackpool's pleasure land protesting against Aldermaston. We had made a big banner with the CND logo, around which we had written 'World in peace, not pieces'. We would listen to Bob Dylan records, and his 'The lonesome death of Hattie Carroll' remains one of my favourite songs. It is a poem. Things were stirring although I wasn't really quite sure what my feelings were. My first vote, of course, was incredibly important. Two of the candidates in my constituency were Harold Wilson and Screaming Lord Sutch – I hope I voted for Harold Wilson.

The next turning point was leaving home and going to

drama school. I was twenty-two and it was the sixties. It was the era of Vietnam and the Industrial Relations Act. We were students, and politics was on the tips of all our tongues. America's involvement in the Vietnam War made us all angry and eventually we were caught up in the famous Grosvenor Square demonstration in 1968. A group broke from the main demonstration and were swept up in fierce clashes of violence with the police outside the American Embassy. I think it was at that point also that I first saw the police in a different way. Until then I had always seen them as people who were there to protect me. For the first time they looked at me and didn't see a human being, just a demonstrator, a disturber of the peace. I got lost in the crowd and was searching desperately for my husband. I wanted their help, but they just pushed me on. I was frustrated and angry. If I 'moved on' I would disappear in the crowd and never find him, I wanted them to understand this, but I met with eyes full of hostility. I realized then that I would always have two relationships with the police – running towards them for help, and running away from them for help.

During this student period Enoch Powell caused controversy with his infamous 'Rivers of Blood' speech. He had made this speech in the Spring of '68 at the AGM of the West Midlands area of the Conservative Political Centre in Birmingham. It was an attack on immigrants to Britain, who he threatened would take 'Englishmen's' jobs, and he inferred that there was a conspiracy amongst Commonwealth immigrants to change the face of England. With sophisticated scare-mongering he said:

'As I look ahead, I am filled with foreboding. Like the Roman, I seem to see "the River Tiber foaming with much blood". That tragic and intractable phenomenon which we watch with horror on the other side of the Atlantic, but which there is interwoven with the history and existence of the States itself, is coming upon us here by our own volition and our own neglect.' These dangerous sentiments were reminiscent of Germany during the Third Reich. His speech of course, like all attacks on minorities, played into the hands of people's prejudices and insecurities.

It was to be the first real bone of contention between myself and my parents on a political level. They had come to visit me in London for the weekend, and as we waited at Euston for their homeward train, we started discussing the issues raised in that speech. I was devastated to discover that my parents were taken in by what he was saying – although now I know they wouldn't be. We all got extremely emotional. And my mother said:

'I don't know what's got into you, you always used to agree with your father.' There was something else my mother said that weekend:

'You should be dressing better now that you're an actress – you've never looked nice since I stopped dressing you.' Were these two comments signs of the umbilical cord being cut?

A sobering summer

DURING MY last year at drama school I spent the summer holidays living with friends in Lincoln. Money not being in great abundance, it became necessary to take a job. How easy it used to be; you needed a job, and there it was. Whether the job I took was everyone's 'cup of tea' remains to be seen.

There was an enormous psychiatric hospital near Lincoln, a beautiful and imposing building, a short bus ride from the city centre. On my first day I wandered down corridors looking for offices, collecting my uniform (a bottle-green overall) and searching for the ward I had been assigned to. At last I found it, the place that was to be 'home' for the next few weeks. I was greeted in the kitchen by Martha, a wholesome rotund octogenarian, who reminded me so much of my Grandma that I immediately felt at home. She welcomed me, put bread in the toaster, and presented me with an overstrong cup of tea. She seemed wrapped in clothes, and wore at least three aprons. As I was biting into my second piece of toast, Sister bounced into the room. Her arrival was something of a shock; as I was being lulled into a sense of homeliness, she immediately reminded me that I was 'here to work'. An inspection of the ward began.

Beyond the kitchen there was a dining room and then a sitting room with not so cosy looking plastic armchairs gathered around the odd table covered with formica. A huge television set took centre stage, suspended from a metal arm attached to the ceiling. On the left of the living area were the bathrooms with the usual toilets, sinks and several very large baths. Further on again was the ward as we understand the meaning of the word, that is rows of beds neatly made, each with its locker neatly placed at the side, like a little army ready for the march. At the far end of this large and airy room was a spectacular bay window overlooking a most surprisingly beautiful garden, which extended to the hospital farm. Besides myself and Sister, who rattled instructions and expectations at me throughout, we were accompanied on 'the tour' by another nurse and a silent woman who seemed to give the appearance of being a nurse. I say this because the uniform just wasn't quite right; to my limited experience I assumed that you probably added more 'bits' to it, the higher up the ladder you got. She was an extremely statuesque woman with a voiceless intensity which I found rather disturbing, particularly as I appeared to be the object of her very penetrating stares. Her hair was black and elegantly forties style – *à la veroiviolate* – smooth and close to her head, then rolled around her face and neck, making a magnificent frame to the handsome features. I was totally wrong about the uniform; she wasn't a nurse, she only thought she was. She was actually an inmate. She followed me for days, eyes boring into my back as I wrestled unsuccessfully with 'hospital corners'.

One morning, after about a week of this unnerving silence, she strode into the kitchen and glared at me, then demanded that I teach her to do the twist. So I did. There, in the white sterile kitchen, to strains of 'Let's twist again' from my toneless voice, we twisted and twirled and a friendship was sealed.

Martha, meanwhile, who was another patient, as you may by now have gathered, continued to greet me at seven in the morning with toast and tea. At coffee breaks she would summon nurses, sisters and any passing doctors into the kitchen (and woe betide anyone who didn't come when they were called). Martha kept the keys to every cupboard and room on a big ring buried somewhere in a pocket in the second layer of apron. Whenever anyone wanted access to the locked premises, Martha would be approached and lifting up her top apron with a flourish she would dive into the hidden pocket and keys would exchange hands. Dear Martha, who had spent forty years in the hospital, firmly believed that it was a hotel, and that she was its

housekeeper, and although sometimes it must have been irritating for the nursing staff to have to get her permission to use the keys, they played the game, for her sanity. For there was no doubt about it, apart from her delusion about the hospital, Martha was perfectly sane. And what kept her sane was the sense of responsibility she was given.

For most of the day the ward would be fairly empty as the patients had work to do in various places in the hospital. Occasionally, patients who were on specific drugs or being prepared for ECG treatment, shock treatment as you probably know it, would sit on chairs, some rocking, some sobbing, mostly in silence. It was very sobering.

There was a lovely woman on the ward, Audrey, about forty, attractive, bubbly. She was always bright and full of humour, and it was hard to decipher what her form of 'madness' could be. One day, while I was assisting a nurse in dishing out the lunch time meal, Audrey lent forward and whispered something to my colleague. A look of wariness came over the nurse's face, then suddenly Audrey lashed out at her.

'He's a bastard!', she yelled, 'look at him, he's a bastard!'

Trays of baked beans and lumpy mash shot across the floor, as the nurse and staff rushed to control her. Amidst struggles and screams she was carted off. Everyone was deeply upset; most of the patients were highly sensitive and it took little to make them cry. I'm a bit sensitive myself, and I was frightened to death. For the rest of my time there Audrey was heavily drugged, standing silently, gazing out of the grand bay window. She was, I learned, a schizophrenic, which had first become apparent when she was jilted at the altar.

I became, at twenty-three, the 'kitchen agony aunt'. I'd always secretly thought the nurses rather hard, so I spent endless hours talking to the women on the ward, listening to their often earth shattering problems. When I took bright, articulate ladies down for their shock treatment, and then later returned them in wheelchairs, shocked and stunned, my heart would break. I went home each evening and relived their problems with anyone who would give me an ear. I couldn't sleep. Their problems were becoming mine. One day I was summoned to Sister's office and given a lecture.

'It's a fine line', she said, 'between them and us; you can be of no use to them at all if you indulge yourself with their problems.'

She was right, of course. I took a step back and became better for it.

Mixed in with all this sadness there was a great deal of humour and warmth. There was lovely Gladys, about sixty years old, extremely attractive and always beautifully made up. She took me to her locker and showed me all her glamorous negligées and lace 'undies', that she was collecting for her bottom drawer. Promiscuous Gladys was always being extracted by the nurses from her fornicating antics 'down on the farm'.

And then there were 'the babies'. A little group of ladies aged about seventy with the mental age of three or thereabouts. I adored them. We all did. They were 'toddlers' in every sense of the word except physically. On first glance, to the unobservant eye they were just a group of rather overweight elderly ladies prone to wearing ribbons in their hair. But as you became accustomed to them, you realized they were quite simply 'toddlers', with the same brightness and originality that you

would encounter in any playgroup across the country.
We bathed them and dressed them, fed them, put
ribbons in their dreadful 'hospital-cut' hair, and waved
them off to work. Two by two, clasping each others'
hands, they'd trundle down the ward, chatting and
giggling, looking forward to the day's activities.
Sometimes one or other of them would decide that she
didn't wish to work that day, and would disappear. I
would find her standing in a corner, back to the room,
with eyes tightly closed – hiding. They were a delight,
and I missed them when I left. It was a special ward and
one I have never forgotten.

When I returned to drama school, the very first play
we were to do was the *Marat Sade* or, to give its full title,
*The Persecution and Assassination of Jean-Paul Marat
as Performed by the Inmates of the Asylum of Charenton
under the Direction of the Marquis de Sade* – an imposing title and an imposing play, written by Peter Weiss.
It had the form of a play within a play, with actors
performing the inmates of Charenton. It was a strange
coincidence, but I think that, owing to the understanding gained from the experience of working in that
hospital, I was able to bring a knowledge and perception
to my part in it that without those patients I could never
have done. I hope I did them justice.

8 *Beginnings*

THE FOLLOWING years for me were more clouded as far as politics were concerned. My attention was grabbed by drama school activity, getting my first job, getting married, getting separated – all these took priority in my life. My first few jobs after leaving drama school had left me rather disillusioned. I felt I was lucky to be working, and because of this had accepted work without discrimination. I started to feel that it was work without depth or substance and I began to flounder. I had seen a lot of the work of Nancy Meckler's Freehold Theatre Company. This was a fringe theatre company that broke new boundaries in presentation. Its work was exciting and stimulating, and seeing its adaptation of *Antigone* remains one of the finest theatrical experiences I have had. I longed for a similar stimulus. The opportunity was soon to come my way.

In the mid- and late sixties many talented actors and directors, partly because of lack of work and partly because of a need to be involved in challenging new work, were forming their own companies. Initially, they worked without funding, until they had proved to the Arts Council that they deserved a grant. In the late 1960s I happily found myself working with one of these companies. It was called Portable Theatre and had recently been set up by David Hare and Tony Bicat. At first we operated from Tony's mother's house off Charlotte Street; in fact, I managed to rent a little room in the house, where most of the other members were already living. We rehearsed in very cold rooms in Mayfair. In retrospect it seems rather a grand way to join a socialist fringe theatre company.

I heard David Hare talking recently on *Desert Island Discs* about these days, recalling how angry we were, tearing round the country getting rid of our anger. I was puzzled by this because I can't honestly remember being all that angry, but I was certainly learning a lot from them, and enjoying myself immensely. David Hare was a lovely director to work with. My first part was Madame in Jean Genet's *The Maids*, which we doubled with a play that David hurriedly wrote for us to complete our repertoire. I am ashamed to say that, considering he is now such a revered playwright, I can't remember what it was called. I felt, for the first time, in control of my work and certainly extremely fulfilled. And through this I was gaining more and more confidence. We had managed to obtain a 'grant-aided' volkswagen touring van, and we did just that – up and down the country we went – visiting universities, colleges, pubs, even rooms. It was often a struggle both to pay wages and gain audiences. When we later toured Howard Brenton's *Christie in Love*, which I was stage managing as it was an all male cast, we played to two people at the Umbrella Club in Coventry. I saw David Hare quite recently and we were reminiscing over those times; he informed me that I would be surprised at how many people insist now that they saw those productions!

If David Hare was 'angry', he never seemed so to me; indeed he was the first 'intellectual socialist' that I had ever met. He was widely read, and had a huge perspective on world politics, in an intellectual way that I had never before encountered, whereas my own politics at that time were rather emotional and built on a sense of injustice. I loved to listen to him, although most of the time I felt out of my depth. It suddenly occurred to me that I had better start reading the right newspapers.

Whilst working for Portable Theatre I had met another young director called Malcolm Griffiths, who had been appointed director of Farnham Repertory Theatre. He asked me to join his company. So, waving goodbye to Portable Theatre, I took up residence in Farnham. One of the reasons I wanted to work for Malcolm, apart from having seen his work, which I admired, was that the company were all on equal wages, not just the actors, but also stage management, production and design. I liked that; at the time it appealed to my sense of right. It was a great company, no stars, no egos; good work. Sadly, I think it was ahead of its time, or perhaps Farnham was the wrong place to be experimenting. Certainly the theatre board were not as enthusiastic as I was, for Malcolm Griffiths's contract was not renewed. And when he went, we went.

I spent a long thoughtful summer working as a barmaid in a very busy riverside pub in London. I had succeeded in doing some good work with good people, which was both progressive and stimulating. But where to now? One of the company members from Farnham had got a job running a new arts centre in London called the Cockpit Theatre. He asked me, while I was out of work, if I would like to open a coffee bar there for him. What started off as an innocent 'filler' job was to change my life.

9

On strike!

THE ARTS CENTRE was well equipped, but modest in its beginnings. Its funding came directly from the ILEA, and most of the work in those days was teacher oriented music and drama groups. One group which impressed me particularly was run by Gordon Wiseman, who was using drama as a method of teaching handicapped children. These kids were amazing, and the workshops they were involved in were so exciting. Their excitement would always run over into the coffee break, and people would have to be rescued from their practical jokes. A theatre director, a rather attractive blonde lady, was one day 'observing' the group. The children – well mainly the boys – were eyeing her intensely. After finishing her coffee, she disappeared to the lavatory. I disappeared to the kitchen. Suddenly there was a great commotion, girls screaming and pointing accusingly, and giggling boys hurtling out of the ladies' toilet, shouting

'We seen it! We seen it!'

When the red-faced visitor emerged it was acutely obvious what they had seen. And these irrepressible children were handicapped; they certainly taught me a thing or two.

The Cockpit grew and flourished and, as it grew, so did the demands on the coffee bar.

'Wouldn't it be nice if we could have snacks?', was the first request I heard, which soon stretched to 'Wouldn't it be nice if we could offer lunches?'.

The Cockpit is situated just off Market Street, which is off the Edgware Road. It had and, indeed, still has a thriving community, lots of pubs and antiques and a busy street market. Somewhere serving lunches would be ideal in this area. Whether the little kitchen I occupied would be equipped to serve up these lunches was another question. But, eager to take up the challenge, I forged ahead. 'Kitchen' was actually a rather flattering word, for it consisted only of a small sink and two electric rings and, if I stretched my arms out, I could touch both walls. I shopped locally from the market stalls; I made soup, lots of salad, and one hot meal a day. And I bought cakes and yoghurt. All morning as I prepared the food, different groups and classes would come to the counter demanding coffee. I became demented. I was rude to the customers. I threw cups at the wall, but still the demand grew, and like a chicken without a head I ran around trying to be all things to all men. Something had to give. And on the day that the director of the centre presented me with thirty touring Germans who ate through everything I had prepared for my regular customers in twenty minutes flat, something did.

The next day customers were not greeted by a sweating snarling chef, but by a darkened coffee bar; without coffee, indeed without life. Except in the corner a large board with a large statement, and myself, sitting bravely reading a copy of *Das Kapital*. My demands were simple: I needed a metal grille in order to close, reasonable hours to serve coffee, and to allow myself time to shop and cook. I was not to be exploited. It

worked. My very first political stand worked. The grille arrived post haste. What power to slam it shut and shout triumphantly 'I am closed!'.

I don't think I ever saw that as a particularly import-ant political turning point. I quite simply felt that I was being treated in an unjust way, and something had to be done. Later I even acquired an assistant!

During the development of my culinary efforts, Gordon Wiseman had been developing his group work. He had, in fact, employed a number of actor–teachers to work with children or young adults, I should say, on set texts for GCE. Their first assignment was to be *Macbeth*. It was a whole day's workshop with fifth year students, exploring the text and presenting scenes from the same. It was hugely successful, and extremely exciting to watch. In my mind then a sort of jigsaw started fitting together. To use theatre in this way – to make Shakespeare so accessible – to be in character improvising on the floor with the kids was fascinating and demanding. Every day when I had finished my washing up I'd creep up to the gallery and ogle the actors, longing for a chance to participate.

My chance came. In long discussions with Gordon Wiseman about his team's work I had 'let slip' that I was an actress. My non-stop enthusing eventually paid off and he invited me down from my spy hole in the gallery to take part in the discussion groups with the kids. So at the end of my session in the kitchen I would rush down to join the actors in the theatre. Soon there was a vacancy in the team, and I begged to be auditioned. Which I was – successfully. And that was the beginning of a new stage in my life. Sue Johnston: actor–teacher.

10

George Best meets
Queen Anne

I SPENT TWO years with the Cockpit Theatre in
Education team, and during that time I think I probably
learnt as much as the kids we worked with. The end of
this period culminated in a day's workshop on Chau-
cer's *Troilus and Criseyde*, where the theatre became,
for that day, the court of King Richard of England. The
programme was for sixth formers and as they entered
the 'mediaeval court' they were presented by name to
the waiting Queen Anne, namely me in a wimple. It was
astonishing how many Master George Bests there were
around in the Middle Ages. The students built, with the
character, the 'mansions', or sets for the actors to perform in. And memorable comments such as 'Madam,
may I borrow your sellotape?', or 'Sire, could I go and
invent tobacco?', became, next to my struggles with olde
English, the highlights of the day. A few months
previous to our beginning this programme, we had
taken part in a festival of children's work. During this I
saw a lecture demonstration which had me rooted to my
seat. It was given by the Coventry Belgrade Theatre in
Education team, the pioneers of this work with children. The demonstration was first rate both in performance and content. I was even more interested because it

embraced all age groups, not just secondary school children, which had been our brief at the Cockpit. That summer found me taking up residence in Coventry, and beginning three of the most fulfilling years of my life so far.

The Belgrade team had that spring of 1973 returned from a successful lecture tour in America. Finding themselves a few thousand pounds richer, they decided to plough the money back into the community by devising a show for older children and adults. The venue for this production was to be a huge marquee on the green outside the main theatre, itself in the centre of Coventry. It was this production that I joined at its concept stage. The idea was that it should be a 'political pantomime': a satire using one of the Christmas 'worthies' as its form, and the antics of the then Heath government, and its effect on the people as its content. We were to devise the piece and David Holman, the resident playwright, would then go away and write it. Suddenly, to be just an actor was not enough; more was required of me and more, certainly, was demanded. I began to feel extremely embarrassed about my limited knowledge of the world in which I lived. I realized that to stand my ground with these people I had chosen to work with, I had to learn, and learn fast. I knew I had been employed mainly for my acting skills, but now I wanted more. I didn't want to feel 'left behind' in their discussions, I didn't want to sit hiding behind a bemused expression, I really did want to understand. I knew I had my work cut out, but it was exciting. It was the Heath government, and the era of increased land value: of Centre Point in London, when the value of property empty was more than that of property filled. Britain was preparing too for the lead up to the eventual referendum to decide on entry into the Common Market, and ROSLA – the raising of the school leaving age – had become law. All this and more, we intended, with music, to pack into our panto. We chose Red Riding Hood as our *tour de force*; the play's full title was *Red Riding Hood and her struggle against the Wolves, like*. I played Red Riding Hood desperate to marry Jack, the militant woodcutter, but a victim of ROSLA, pining away another year in the classroom, and granny in the forest, a victim of capitalism, under pressure from the wolves to sell her cottage to enable them to build high-rise flats. I can recall only one problem during the whole of the run, and that was the nightly visits of 'the phantom crapper' as he lovingly became known. He would leave his mark every night, and it would be discovered in the morning by the stage manager, when he put his foot in it. It was an unusual show to begin with, and certainly by the end of it I had gained a lot more information and understanding of the politics of my country and the nocturnal habits of one of the nocturnal residents of Coventry. I had also begun to realize the extremes of discord on the Left, but that's something I will come back to later.

11 *Pow Wow*

ONE OF THE programmes contained in the demonstration that had so impressed me was for infants. It was called *Pow Wow* and now, with Red Riding Hood behind us, it went into infants' school, and I was keen to see it in performance with children. I was not to be disappointed.

Pow Wow is a participation programme devised for one class of infants aged six to seven years. It is important to stress that the children were to be involved as themselves in this programme and *not* as an audience in the given sense of the word. Also, it was important not to overweight them with adults: too many adults and the children would start looking to them for guidance. The aim was for *them* to make the decisions, so visitors to the class were limited, usually to two.

Myself, and the other visitor on this particular day went into the classroom a good twenty minutes before the show was due to begin. I was introduced to the children by the teacher as a school visitor and then I faded away to a discreet corner of the room. The children were involved in ordinary classroom activity. There were no signs of any impending drama, no unusual buzz of excitement, simply a poster on a wall near the door advising us that 'Tex's Wildwest Show'

was about to 'hit town'. Suddenly the door opened and
Tex did just that – he hit us! It was so unexpected, even
for me, that thirty little mouths and three even larger
ones gaped wide open. He was six foot six inches, this
cowboy – huge even to me. So, standing there, dressed
all in black, hat tipped back, he must have seemed like a
colossus to these little people around me.

'Hi', he drawled in his easy Texan accent.

' 'Allo', they responded in their Coventry ones.

Tex had arrived, and he was to perform his show for
them that very morning in the school hall. There followed half an hour's chat with the children. He was
glamorous and exciting. He perpetuated the myth of the
'all American gun-slinging' cowboy, travelling across
America and fighting off all those 'sneaky, pesky
Injuns'. By the end of the session he was 'Super Hero',
and the Indian was everything we had always been led
to believe in Western movies: a fearsome ruthless beast
with whom your scalp was not safe. We also learned
that in the school hall he had a 'real live Injun' in a 'real
teepee'. We gasped. But were reassured, everything
was 'Okay, because he is in a lil ol' cage. So if yawl
stand', he swaggered to the door, 'we can all go and see
the show.' As we rose to our feet, a shocked expression
crossed his face, and we were told to sit down again
immediately. Taking the teacher to one side, he stage
whispered in her ear,

'These kids look kinda small. How old are they?' And
she told him.'I think there's been a mistake, Ma'am', he
said, 'I only do this show for eight year olds, these kids
are kinda young.'

Disappointment hung in the air. He returned to the
children, his eyes moving from one child to another.

'They do look kinda tough', he said ruminatively.

Eyes looked more hopeful, 'Kinda smart. You wanna go see my show?'

'Yes!', they cried as one.

'Well, Ma'am', he said, turning back to the teacher, 'would you take responsibility?'

'Yes', she said quietly, 'I will.'

Great relief all around, and armed with this new vision of ourselves as 'strong and tough', we scuttled into rows, and waited by the door to visit the formidable 'Injun'. On arrival in the hall, a spectacular sight met our eyes: there at the far end was a giant teepee or wigwam. Made out of soft skins and decorated with authentic symbols and paintings, it looked as real as anything you could find this side of Arkansas. Furs and rugs were draped across the floor, and a tall spear was propped against the side of the teepee, its head shining and glinting in the sunlight. Surrounding it was a cage, with a door at the front, locked with an extremely sturdy padlock, ensuring our 'safety'. Of the Indian there was no sign.

'Sit down', commanded Tex. We sat where we were – a very comfortable distance away from the cage, and no amount of charming persuasion from Tex could make us move closer. Tex strode across the hall, and shouted an order. The door of the teepee was flung back, and there, framed in the blackness, was the Indian. Once again, thirty-three mouths were wide open: he was magnificent. He was dressed from head to foot in animal skins, with fringing on his pants, and moccasins on his feet. The crowning glory, covering his glossy black hair and cascading his full length, was a resplendent Indian chief's headdress that every seven-year-old child would die for – although perhaps not this particular group at this particular time! The show began.

The Indian was put through his paces. Tex told the story that we all suspected was true: the savage Indian eating his food from the ground, sleeping on the ground, hunting and killing animals; and hunting and killing the 'white man'. The war paint was smeared on and the Indian told to dance the war dance. Throughout the show the Indian's reluctance to perform had become increasingly obvious. And that he had no love of his 'superior' was equally obvious. Now, at the point of the dance, the Indian stopped and was defiantly staring at Tex with eyes full of loathing.

'Dance', ordered Tex. No reaction. Just a slow grudging stare.

'Dance', again came the command. And again the resistance. Tex's right hand hovered above his gun, and in a flash it was drawn and spun and pointed at the Indian's head.

'Dance', he spat. And the Indian danced.

The children squirmed and positions changed a little. Our friend the cowboy had shown another side: hard, angry, rather austere. The sight of him now, with his gun in his hand, compared awesomely with the sight of the humiliated Indian, dancing piteously around his jail, at the point of a gun. The show ended and the Indian returned willingly to the security of his home. We prepared to leave the hall. But Tex was deep in conversation with the teacher, and he seemed anxious and agitated. We were soon offered an explanation. Apparently there had been some confusion over his bookings for the next performance, he must use the school phone and sort out the mess. The teacher instructed us to stay where we were, while she directed Tex to the phone. We all sat cross legged at the furthest end of the hall and stared at the silent teepee. There was a movement and the flap across the door was thrown back; the Indian reappeared. Children gasped and inched back a little. He, however, hardly looked our way, just shot us a cursory glance, and then began a slow inspection of his home. There was a hole high up on the right side of the tent. He searched around his cage and found a piece of cloth but it was too small. We watched in silence. And then suddenly and oh so unexpectedly he spoke: a deep, deep sound, guttural, short; and unidentifiable. He looked at us fully then, and sixty-six saucer eyes looked back at him. Moving to the front of the cage, he gripped the bars in his great hands, and looked searchingly around the hall. He alone moved, we were stuck to the floor. Then his eyes rested on a large piece of cloth lying at the side of the room – our side of the room. All heads turned and saw the cloth, then all heads turned back to him. The Indian went back to the hole and then, that voice again, in broken simple words, and with the use of a little mime, explained why he needed the cloth. As he mimed the rain falling down and into his home, he asked the children:

'How you call?'

'Rain', responded the children.

'Rain', he said with satisfaction, 'rain.' Then he came forward again, 'Me Black Elk', he announced. 'You help Black Elk.' No response, just a shifting of weight. He looked again at the cloth he needed: 'You give Black Elk.'

Silence. You could eat the tension. He looked at us and we all looked back. And then a young boy, who seemed so small, ran from the group, grabbed the cloth, flung it over the cage and ran back to us. Still no one spoke. Black Elk stooped down and, taking the cloth, returned to the teepee, and began his task. And while he worked, he talked to the children. He told them about his real teepee at home in north America, how the one they could see was not real, just one Tex had had made for the show. Tex, it seemed, had taken everything from him. We learned of the Indian way of life, and the white man coming. All the time the children were edging closer – closer, just a little closer – to the cage. He told his stories in his faltering English, and when he couldn't find the words, the children would provide. He began to tell of his Indian village, and then abruptly he stopped. Why tell them, when he could show them. Would they like to make an Indian village like his? Would they like to hunt the buffalo? Would they? Yes, yes.

'Then you must let Black Elk out of the cage.'

That hadn't been anticipated; that was different. Suddenly they retreated, shuffling on little bottoms back to safety.

'You no trust Black Elk?', he questioned.

'No', they whispered.

He strode angrily back across his space and grabbed the awesome spear. 'Who trust Black Elk?', he demanded. Again the little boy, the one who had rushed for the cloth, rose to his feet. But not so fast this time.

'You come.' The Indian beckoned. The small boy cautiously approached the side of the cage. The spear was passed through the bars into small trembling hands and, kneeling, Black Elk placed the spearhead against his own throat.

'How you call', he said to the boy.

'Philip', he croaked.

'Black Elk trust Philip.' And putting his hands behind his back, and with the spear at his throat, he instructed the boy to push. Wide eyed, Philip pushed, not hard, but he knew the power he had.

'Good', said Black Elk, retrieving the spear. 'Now you trust Black Elk.'

Brave little Philip, standing there, while this 'wild savage' pointed the weapon at his throat. No one moved or spoke. We just watched with baited breath.

Then it was over. Philip grinned at Black Elk. Black Elk grinned back. They shook hands. Everyone laughed in relief.

'Now you open cage', again demanded Black Elk. And led by Philip the children undid the padlock and set him free.

They built their village. Miraculously Black Elk found enough sticks to build several small skeleton teepees. He found a length of blue silk which became the river and a magnificent black fur which he threw over the teacher and, having taught us his skills for trapping the buffalo, we 'hunted' her around the hall. Then we sat down for a 'Pow Wow'.

It was then he decided to share a secret with us. He stressed the importance of our never disclosing what he was about to tell. It seemed that when Tex robbed him of all his possessions Black Elk managed to save two things: his tomahawk and his pipe of peace. Would we like to see them? Of course we would. From a hidden place at the back of the teepee, he fetched a bundle which he unwrapped to reveal a splendid tomahawk, and a strange, delicate looking pipe. He held them almost tenderly and passed them round for inspection, warning us of the dangers of the razor sharp small axe. When they were back in his possession, he demonstrated the effectiveness of the tomahawk by hurling it into a block of wood. There it stuck very deep in the wood, the handle shuddering. We smoked the pipe of peace, sitting cross legged in a circle, passing it from one to another – all at peace, all content.

The door burst open and there was Tex! Eyes blazing. 'What the hell's going on here', he bellowed.

Children shot to their feet and, gathering in a bunch in front of him, they turned to look at the Indian and gasped in fear. For in his hand he held the dreadful tomahawk. They turned back to Tex, and there in his hand was a large black gun. The two men faced each other, eyes locked, weapons pointed, and between them the children, transfixed.

Tex broke the mood. He suggested they both put their weapons down. They did so slowly, and we watched in silence as they laid them at their feet. Tex demanded to know where the tomahawk and pipe had come from. And the children told him.

'I'm a fair man', drawled Tex. 'You can decide what happens. If you want him to keep his things and go free, then that's the way it will be. But if you think *I* should have them, then he must go back into the cage and my show will go on.'

Grown-ups were removed from the group and instructed to stand against the wall. Tex and Black Elk dropped back a few yards away, still watching each other across the heads of the children.

'When I say', said Tex, 'move towards the person you want to keep the things.' He paused for a moment; we waited. Then the instruction came.

'Move.'

The children set off, surprisingly quickly, it seemed to me, the majority of them without hesitation; several of them dithered, wanting to go one way, but seeing the bulk of their friends going in the other direction, they changed their minds. All except one little boy, young Philip, who strode over and stood alone at the side of his saddened friend. Together they looked across the floor at the class grouped around Tex.

I was amazed. So was the teacher. Then Tex whipped into action. He marched across the wooden floor grabbing Black Elk's treasured possessions as he went.

'Back in the cage', he rapped, 'then get that teepee down and packed away. We've got another show to do today.' We were taken from the hall and, glancing back, we caught a last sight of the Indian, head bowed, beginning to pack away Tex's belongings, while Tex sat admiring his new acquaintance.

When we returned to the classroom I couldn't resist asking a group of the children why they had chosen the cowboy.

'He had the gun', a few volunteered.

Theatrically the programme had ended; now the teacher had her role to play. Teachers had been heavily involved with the actors throughout. Workshop meetings had been attended and a performance, or part of one, had already been seen. A teacher's pack, with ideas for follow-up material, had been prepared and would now be in their possession. But for me it was the discussions that were to follow that were important.

The children had been through an experience where real emotional and intellectual demands had been made of them. I know there are people who feel that it is undesirable or even dangerous for young children to be involved in such a powerful emotional situation. I really believe that we should never underestimate the levels of understanding that children can bring even to complex issues. It has been my experience, working in Theatre in Education for so many years, that teachers have been continually amazed at the depth of their own children's responses to and involvement in challenging material.

The quality of our work at Coventry was always something we strived for; we preferred to work closely with small numbers of children wherever finance would allow. And it is with a sense of pride that I look back at my work there. I also remember it as a period of enormous struggle for all of us who were in the company at that time. I think that this struggle came out of the fact that we were a democratic company, all of us with equal responsibility and commitment, all of us strong minded and determined to express our own under-standing of the world. Because our policy was to reflect this 'real world' in which we lived – no Flopsy Bunny here – it was important that we ourselves understood that 'real world' and, being of different experiences and political persuasions, this would often lead to hours of heated debate and passionate discussions.

It was a period of struggle for me. I found it hard to comprehend some of the extreme left policies I was hearing for the first time. And in some instances seeing the truth in what I was being told frightened me and made me resist, desperately wanting to believe in 'good old England', and the sanctuary and comfort I felt as a child when politics had not entered my life. There were several of us who resisted and, feeling ourselves out on a limb, we formed our own group, 'The Pink Wallies'. It gave us courage to face some of the rather hard line approaches we felt were coming into our company meet-ings. Sometimes the political drifts between us would produce untold tensions, occasionally bordering on hysteria; climbing into a van at eight o'clock for a performance in school to hear that 'our brothers in Argentina were having a bit of a hard time' or to the strains of an improvised song, 'Smash the system, take the factories: they're yours', almost led Maggie Steed and myself to nervous breakdowns. But when it got this bad, which, I hasten to add, wasn't often, common sense would prevail and things shifted back into perspective. Then I could see that it was the dogma that I was resisting and not the principles behind it. Out of all this conflict came learning and understanding. Sometimes I felt as if I were a child, participating in *Pow Wow*, being emotionally stretched and challenged, and having to make choices; and all the time growing and learning.

12 The case of Craig and Bentley

ONE DAY we were to have a devising meeting for a new top secondary programme we were due to produce. A few people put ideas on the table, but none of them was particularly inspiring any of us into action. Then Harry Miller told us the story of Craig and Bentley.

On the evening of 2 November 1952, nineteen-year-old Derek Bentley, an epileptic with the mental age of eleven, was watching television with his parents, William and Lillian Bentley, when there was a knock at the door. It was his friend, sixteen-year-old Christopher Craig. Derek's mother sent him on his way. For a long time she and her husband had been unsuccessfully trying to end the association between this boy and their son Derek. A little later there was another knock at the door and there stood a more impressive friend, a well spoken grammar school boy, Norman Parsley. Derek followed this boy to the street corner and there waiting for him was Craig. And as the two set off to Croydon together, destiny began to take control of their lives.

Their aim that night was to break into a butcher's shop, but on arrival they discovered it was occupied. An attempt to break into an electrical shop was also thwarted. Their last attempt was a warehouse. They climbed over a gate into the alleyway, but could find no way in. Craig then led Bentley via a climb up the drainpipe, on to the roof. What they were not aware of was that their antics had been observed by a nine-year-old girl, who informed her father; he set off to tell the police.

During the bus ride from Norbury to Croydon, Craig had handed Bentley a knuckle duster he had made, which Bentley pocketed, alongside the knife he already carried. Craig had a gun. Bentley's possible knowledge of this was to play a fundamental part in the resulting analysis of the night's events. Now trapped up on the roof with no means of escape, just a lift shaft to retreat behind, the two friends became aware of movement and voices. Looking down they were amazed to see policemen in the gardens below. What followed is now history.

With the arrival of the police on the roof, Bentley came out from behind the lift shaft and gave himself up. Then, in the custody of the policeman, he is alleged to have shouted, 'Let him have it, Chris.' Whereupon Craig produced a gun and shot at Detective Constable Fairfax. Fairfax, not seriously injured, but shocked, searched Bentley, who had stayed beside him and, expecting to find a gun, found only the knife and knuckle duster.

'That's all I've got, sir', Bentley told him, 'I haven't a gun.'

By now more police had arrived, some finding it difficult to scale the thirty-foot drain pipe, and entry by any other means had been delayed while they waited for the arrival of the keys to the door to the roof. It was through this door that Police Constable Miles burst and was shot dead, a bullet between the eyes.

Bentley, who had been under arrest for fifteen minutes when this event took place, was taken down the stairs and removed from the scene in the back of a police car.

More shots were fired, then Craig, seeing defeat, held his gun to his head and fired twice – the gun didn't go off. And, seizing the opportunity, Fairfax advanced on him. It was then that Craig rushed to the edge of the roof and threw himself off. His body hit the greenhouse below and bounced to the ground. He left the scene in the back of an ambulance.

Both boys were found guilty of murder. Christopher Craig, being only sixteen, was to be 'detained at Her Majesty's pleasure'; Derek Bentley, at nineteen, was to be hanged, as indeed he was, on the morning of 28 January 1953.

As Harry reached the climax of the story, we were silent. Then came the question that was at the forefront of everyone's mind. How could it be – how could it be that a boy who was under arrest and who had not shot the policeman could be sentenced and hanged?

Obviously there were facts that we were not privy to. But with Harry feeding us more information we realized that here was a case that could be very relevant to children of the same age as Craig and Bentley, especially when capital punishment had again become a subject for debate owing to the recent IRA bombings in Coventry and Birmingham.

Listening to Harry's story fired me with a need to know more about the case; a need to answer the question, how could it be? I was disturbed, for intuitively I felt that somewhere there could have been a miscarriage of justice, and I was keen to find out the truth.

Marje and me, taking a
break from the 'Saints'.

The sixties look.

1968, the drama student.

Rare Earth part two: 'Drink the Mercury'. The effects of mercury poisoning begin to show themselves. The mother tests her daughter's sight.

Pow Wow. Mike Kay (Tex), David Swapp (Black Elk) and the children as themselves.

Me as Mrs Bronowski, the Polish musician from
Auschwitz in *No Pasoran*.

'Tell me Clare, is that the
actor who plays Cecil
Parkinson?'. Clare Short
MP and me at the House of
Commons, 1989.
Lesley Thomson

The Miners' Wives. l to r:
Joyce, me and Madge.
Lesley Thomson

Edie McCardle. None the worse for the 'kipper experience'.
Lesley Thomson

l to r: Mum, me, Auntie Ena, Pauline, Auntie Milly. Inset: the missing Marjorie.
Lesley Thomson

Drama queen at Clause 28 rally in Manchester, 1988.
Paul Herrmann

We had a new writer working with us at that time, and once we had decided that this was the story we would be pursuing, his brief was to go away and research, and then write a play. We would then rehearse it and take it into schools. It was a new departure for us, since usually the writer had worked with the devising team, but we felt it worth the experiment; sadly, it failed.

All of us who were to be involved in the play had been so enthused by Harry's story that we had started to track down as much information as we could on the subject. The trial transcripts themselves would have stood alone as a dramatic piece. And William Bentley's book, *My Son's Execution*, was deeply moving. But it was *To Encourage the Others* (1971) written by David Yallop, that made me realize that we had hold of a case whose significance we had not fully appreciated. Yallop's book is an extraordinary piece of research, and takes the form of an open letter to the then Home Secretary, Sir David Maxwell Fyfe. I recently had occasion to read the book again and what I find astounding is that the questions raised in this book remain untried, untested and, more importantly, unanswered.

By the time the play was delivered for rehearsal we actors had so much information at our finger tips that it was impossible for the material to live up to our expectations. We felt it was too sentimental and with two weeks to go we made the decision to start again. We would put together our own script through improvisation, on the floor with the writer and with anyone else who was free to contribute. On reflection it seems a lunatic decision, but so fired were we with enthusiasm and commitment to the story that we would not be deterred.

We had to find a form that the kids would relate to. The most obvious, of course, was to just tell the story: for them to become acquainted with the facts, let the events unfold, and for the questions to be raised without prejudice. Derek Bentley was to be our central character and Harry Miller, whose passion for the story was as intense as mine, was ideal casting to play the part. It was also important to give the kids a sense of history; the play had to be set among the violence and discontent of those late forties and early fifties when police morale was low owing to the amount of armed attacks on members of the force. And so we proceeded and, as we did so, the facts of the case unravelled. As they did, for me came the realization that the great British system of justice which I had always accepted as infallible was not only *fallible* and subject to discrepancies but, in the face of an unjust or at the very least controversial judgement, intractable. It taught me that nothing must be accepted at face value, but must be questioned, and whenever I felt a situation or issue to be unjust, it must be challenged.

To cover the case fully in this book would be wrong, for David Yallop has already successfully done this in his book. But I feel I must quote Lord Chief Justice Goddard's summing up at the trial.

> When two people are engaged on a felonious enterprise, and warehouse breaking is a felony — and one knows that the other is carrying a weapon, and there is an agreement to use such violence as may be necessary to avoid arrest, and this leads to a killing of a person, both are guilty of murder.

This is what condemned Bentley. To my mind, and

certainly to David Yallop's, it was never satisfactorily proved. Also, it is interesting to note that the jury's 'guilty with recommendation to mercy' was never called into play. Indeed, in a quote to David Yallop years later Lord Goddard was to say:

> Yes, I thought Bentley was going to be reprieved. He certainly should have been. There is no doubt whatsoever in my mind. Bentley should have been reprieved.

There is no doubt in my mind either that he should have been reprieved.

A few years later I was to meet Derek's sister, Iris; her parents having died, it was left to her to clear Derek's name. And to this day the campaign continues.

Eventually our programme was finished; it was to be a full day's event in school. We felt that in the afternoon, after the performance in the morning, we should have a workshop to investigate some of the issues raised in the play. The play itself, I am pleased to say, proved to be powerful and moving. After lunch we changed direction completely. We had just begun a discussion, all seated on the floor in the hall, when suddenly from amongst the audience a fight erupted. It was fast and furious and over before the kids had time to think. It involved all the actors who had taken part in the show, and in reality was a carefully constructed fight with a purpose. We asked the children to write down exactly what had just happened there, right in front of their eyes. And then with their statements in front of them, we re-enacted in slow motion exactly what had happened. The discrepancies were enormous, as indeed had been all the police evidence given at the trial about exactly what happened that night on the warehouse roof. Needless to say, it made a point.

Finally the young people were divided into small groups, where they were able to 'meet' and question some of the characters from the play. And then once again as a whole group they put questions to the trial judge, Lord Goddard. Through all these questionings they began to perceive how evidence is often open to individual interpretation. I used to enjoy this part of the performance: the children would rise to their feet in anger and frustration at the judge's unbending rendition of the law.

13

'Oi must have blud tonaight, Jgor!'

IN THE AUTUMN of 1976, after I had been at Coventry for three years, I was offered a job with the Bolton Octagon Theatre in Education Company, a company we had always had close association with and whose policy was very similar to our own. It was smaller than ours, but one whose work I admired. Feeling the need for new stimulus, I decided to accept the job, and my re-emergence in the northwest began.

The first production I was to be involved in was in fact a touring play for children and adults called *Fangs*. This was a spoof on the Dracula films. As much as I loved working in TIE, it was a welcome relief to pick up a script already written and just to concentrate on the characterization of my role: Dr Zatopeck. The story was based on the idea that Dracula, under the protection of his faithful servant, Igor, while under sail from Transylvania to destination unknown, had hit upon bad weather in the English Channel, and been washed up on the beach at Blackpool. And from there the story unravelled.

It was great fun for both us and, hopefully, the audience, although I often suspected that we were having more of a hilarious time on stage. Dracula was played by an Irish actor called Eugene Geasley who, and here I hope I don't offend, was about five feet high. Anyway, let us say, he was an extremely small Dracula. He also doubled as the ship's cook, Boris. Eugene had been an escapologist with the Ken Campbell Road Show, and during a part of the play, when he was supposed to be sleeping, he would in full view of the audience, manage completely to change his clothes. We never knew what to expect, and one time when he appeared in the arms of the six-foot-six Clive Russell wearing nothing but red underpants and a pair of wellingtons, I had to leave the stage with two pages of dialogue unspoken.

During the tour, Eugene taught Nick Maloney, another actor in the company, some of the tricks of the escapology trade. One afternoon they decided to per-

form them to the unsuspecting residents of Preston. We arrived in the town centre just in time to see the two of them being unceremoniously bundled into the back of a police car and driven away. They were arrested under the Vagrancy Act for obstruction of the highway, and locked in a cell. We began to panic; in an hour's time we had a matinee to do for 350 children. Mike Kay, the director, desperately pleaded on behalf of the 350, but only when he threatened to bring the children to Dracula did it have any effect. The two thespians were released.

By the time this tour had ended, I felt very well integrated into the company, and ready to start the 'serious' work again. Little did we know what was waiting for us back at base.

14

They shall not pass

First they came for the Jews
and I did not speak out –
because I was not a Jew.
Then they came for the communists
and I did not speak out –
because I was not a communist.

Then they came for the trade
unionists and I did not speak out –
because I was not a trade unionist.
Then they came for me –
and there was no one left
to speak out for me.

Pastor Niemoeller

IN THE mid-seventies came the beginning of the education cuts. Theatre in Education companies all over the country had already been cut, or were under threat. They were seen by some education authorities, extremely misguidedly in my opinion, to be the 'icing on the cake'. And although Bolton had had its team for a good many years, and had tremendous support from teachers, head teachers, and educationalists in the town, the decision was made to axe us. Obviously we did everything we could to get the authorities to reverse this decision, but they were adamant. Strangely enough, we had already been awarded an Arts Council grant for that year, so we decided that we would devise a play that we could tour and 'sell' to other authorities. And while our grant lasted we would look around for a more enlightened authority which might adopt us.

But what to do? We needed to find a programme that would still reflect our policies, but it had also to be marketable. It was while we were involved in these discussions that a teacher approached us with a suggestion that solved our problem.

In Bolton at that time, and indeed in other places across the country, members of the National Front were campaigning and gaining support. This teacher had been horrified one evening, leaving school, to find the NF recruiting at the school gates, and many children were in possession of leaflets which were beginning to fuel racism. Some of you may have seen them for yourselves. They carried illustrations of a gorilla's brain, and other related species' brains, and a black man's brain. And yes, you've guessed it, according to this leaflet the black man's was the smallest.

Despicable and dangerous.

Children, with their limited experience, could never understand the implications of laughing at those pathetic drawings.

What the play's content should be was becoming apparent: we would investigate fascism. We would show the rise of it and the effects of it. And what better example than the rise of fascism in Germany in the thirties, and how Adolf Hitler and his racism could lead to the massacre of six million Jews. It was a heavy subject, and the trouble was how to present it in such a way that we could grab the interest of children of fifteen and upwards. For instance, how important was it to bring in the economic decline of Germany in the late twenties which sowed the seeds for the growth of Hitler. It is obviously extremely important historically, but did the kids need all that information in order to understand fascism? Or was it something that could be used in follow-up material by history teachers? It was probably more important that the kids see the impact of Nazi rule on one character and how it affected and changed his or her life.

At this time I was again working with David Holman, our resident playwright. If there's anything David loves more than children and animals, it's sport, and the use of sport of one sort or another seems to creep into many of his plays. And of course it was successful, for it is a great source of identification for kids of all ages. So it was to sport that he turned again, this time to boxing. It was decided that our central character would be Jan Goldberg, a young Jewish boxer with great potential and, at the beginning of our play, fighting in the ring for Germany. The children would become familiar with this character and follow his life as the Nazi party came to power. We felt it to be important also to show that fascism was not something solely invented by Germany, and that we should bring it home to England and show the emergence of Oswald Mosley and his Blackshirts. But how to bring Jan's character into that? By using sport as a theme we had found the ideal way.

One of the horrifying things about Hitler's regime was how the ordinary people turned a blind eye to the atrocities that were going on around them. Their new found pride in national socialism and the Aryan race, with its promises of a great future, presumably helped them to ignore these things. Or maybe always at the back of their minds was the Gestapo and the fear of the concentration camps. As Jews then communists, Catholics, socialists and homosexuals disappeared it must have become very easy to accept the new regime with enthusiasm. In 1936 the Olympic games were held in Germany and this was ideal for our story, for the reality behind the facade of those games could be shown.

Jan Goldberg, then, was to represent the Jews living in Germany at that time. Although our play was his story, with the use of slides and a large screen over the set, we were able to show the audience what was happening in the outside world.

Jan was no longer allowed to box – certainly he was not allowed to represent Germany; that would have been unthinkable. Along with all other Jews in 1935 he had been deprived of German citizenship, not just stripped of the title of which he had been so proud. He now found it difficult to find a gym that would allow him access. Signs all over Berlin were restricting his freedom as an individual: *Juden unerwuenscht* (Jews not welcome) appeared outside many shops, hotels, beer gardens and places of public entertainment. This was not unlike South Africa today with its *whites only* instructions and, on a less official scale, here, where you see daubed on shop shutters or walls, *Pakis out*, *Blacks go home*.

In 1936 in Berlin, in preparation for the games, and as an opportunity for Germany to impress the world with its achievements, these signs were rapidly removed. Two 'token' Jewish champions were brought back to Germany to stand alongside their German counterparts.

It was a very despondent Jan who, hanging around a

gym one day, got the chance to spar with the English boxing team. And it was through the relationship that developed between them, that the audience saw the reality of living under that fascist regime. Not only were Jews at that time in the main unable to find employment, having been excluded since 1933 from public office, the civil service, teaching, journalism, farming, then later in 1938, from practising the law, but they were also denied the necessities of life, with signs now restricting their entry to food shops and chemists: *Jews not admitted*, *Jews enter this town at their own risk* and, outside a town called Ludwigshafen, was a sign that read: *Drive carefully! Sharp bend. Jews 75 miles an hour*.

These were things that the British team learned, this and other persecutions were exposed to them, all hidden under the great facade of the Berlin Olympics. During the games there was a memorable incident that we featured in the play, and one which I enjoyed immensely. Jesse Owens, the black American athlete, had already taken three gold medals in field events. Hitler had declined to present the medals to him. In the long jump, an 'Aryan' athlete, Lutz Long, was to jump for Germany and, indeed, was favourite for the gold. Hitler was again present watching with interest. Jesse Owens, who had never trained for this event, was the main opposition. Lutz Long, jumping before him, broke the world record by clearing twenty-five feet, ten inches. Then came Owens, hurtling towards the jump, his strong athletic legs striding down the grass and taking him up and beyond Long's mark to twenty-six feet, five-and-a-half inches. Another gold for America. And as all heads turned towards Mr Hitler, he was seen rapidly leaving the arena. By the end of the games Jan's friendship with the British was consolidated, and he was persuaded to return with them to England. And return with them he did, only to walk into Oswald Mosley's Blackshirts and the famous battle of Cable Street, when the British working class fought back against Mosley's movement and, with shops barricaded, London's East End became a battleground; fascism in England, if not eradicated, was at least held in check.

As news of events in Germany escalated, and with the outbreak of war, Jan returned to Germany and, eventually, like six million other Jews, 'disappeared'.

It was essential that we learned what had happened to him. It was important to show the young audience that when hate and prejudice are allowed to take full hold, what the inevitable results of that will be. Hitler had said that Germany had six million unemployed, and six million Jews, an easy equation to feed people's insecurity. How often have you heard here, in Britain, at the height of severe unemployment, 'Blacks and Asians are taking our jobs'?

The ultimate in the persecution of the Jews, of course, was the concentration camps and the gas chambers. How any human being could actually sit down and plan such an operation is incredible. How people could stand by and see men, women and children led from cattle wagons to their unsuspecting deaths is dreadful to conceive. But out of hatred, feeding on fear and prejudice, it happened.

In the play, Sammy McAvoy, one of our English boxers, finds himself back in Germany at the end of the war. He has been making desperate attempts to discover what has happened to Jan. Finally, he sits reading the death lists while a young Jewish violinist who, during her imprisonment at Auschwitz, had played in an orchestra of young Jewish girls, speaks. They played outside the gas chambers, another ploy by the Nazis to maintain calm. She is about to give evidence in the Nuremberg Trials, and as she is taken through it with a solicitor, Sammy listens and learns of the horror. He realizes, as we all do, what Jan's fate would have been.

This show did have an impact on our audience. It is, indeed, an incredible story. I only wish that the world could learn, and at the end of any performance, you could say, 'We learned from this, and of course it will never happen again'. By teaching our children the right values we hope it won't, but sadly one day a group of children coming from a Jewish school to see this production were badly beaten up.

We must always be aware of the dangers. It is important that we are all aware of what man is capable of. There is no bigger example than this of man's inhumanity to man. During the Spanish Civil War, when the people fought the fascists, they had banners and on those banners the words *No pasoran* (They shall not pass) were written. We named our play *No Pasoran*.

15 *Passion*

IT WAS DURING the three years I worked at Coventry that I became involved with union activity and, every year in late March or early April, we Equity members – but never enough of us – would make the pilgrimage to London for our annual general meeting. I have often thought it a great pity that Equity AGMs were not televised, for I believe the general public would find them extremely entertaining.

There are many political differences within our union, which frequently lead to high-level arguments and very bitter debate. These, interspersed with more theatrical offerings, and unequalled quips from the floor, have made me feel, often despairingly, that I have attended some bizarre carnival instead of a meeting where decisions have been made that could affect the livelihoods of our membership.

The meetings have changed somewhat over the years. They always take place during a Sunday and Monday in spring, and in one of our West End theatres. When I first started going, in the early seventies, people would trickle in on a Sunday morning carrying sandwiches, flasks, Sunday papers, babies and dogs; it was very much a family affair. We would read our way through the colour supplements while the voice from the stage droned on through standing orders. It was a time to catch up with old friends, hear their news, spot the famous, and listen to the better debates. But as warnings of theatre closures and Arts Council cutbacks began to build, so did our intensity over Equity's position. Our conferences began to change; if I could use one word to describe those AGMs through the seventies, it would be 'passion'. Two of the main bones of contention at that time were the amalgamation of the three entertainments unions – the actors, the technicians and the musicians – and the formation of the union into a branch and delegate structure. The Left of course was for both, the Right dead against, and a large number of people in the middle didn't know what they wanted.

Every year and with increasing intensity, we would discuss these issues, and almost every year they would be passed in the meeting by the membership, only to fall later when Council would decide that the decision was not in the best interests of the membership, or would put it to a referendum, where it usually failed. The heat of the discussion that greeted these items on the order sheet was beyond belief, most particularly in the case of the branch and delegate structure. What is normal practice to other unions became absolute anathema to an awful lot of Equity members. If you were in favour, in some people's opinion, you must be a communist – a Red. Or, if you were known to them, misguided. I remember sitting in the theatre circle in the midst of one of these furores, and as a well-known actor finished his speech in favour of the motion and left the platform, a behatted lady sitting knitting behind us commented to her friend, whose nose was buried deep in a book, 'Such a pity, so talented too. They go to Russia on these package holidays, and come back with their heads full of these wild ideas.'

'Yes', replied her friend, 'and the food isn't very good either.'

Such was the intensity of feeling over the branch and delegate structure that often when it came to a close result at the vote, a recount would be demanded. At one meeting, when it got to the fifth recount (it was, I might add, an extremely close vote), it was decided that all those voting for should sit on one side of the theatre, and all those against on the other. There followed several minutes of struggle as a theatre completely full of people attempted to move, collecting babies, papers, dogs, children etc. The chaos was great. But I think *we* won the vote. On another occasion, again on the same issue, the debate had completely broken down, abuse was being hurled from stage to floor, and all around was bedlam. There was a brief silence for just a moment,

and then a voice bellowed, 'Great hairy bollocks!' The anger was diffused and humour restored.

Often though, humour was lacking. The object of most people's fury was the policies of the Workers' Revolutionary Party. Personally, I always felt rather sad that the WRP had to end a lot of its motions with the added comment, '... and the nationalization of the entertainments union, banks etc. under workers' control and without compensation'.

Sad quite simply because I thought that ultimate statement was a huge one to pose to people in that situation and, although I could understand why it had to be there, other people couldn't. It operated as a red rag to a bull on motions that otherwise would have seemed sensible, so that they were invariably rejected. It often led to antagonism when clear leadership was needed. Their analysis could be spot on, and some of their predictions have certainly come true, but expecting ordinary people to take the leap into revolution, from their knitting, when most of us were desperately trying to understand the fundamentals of the running of the union, was diversionary.

For my own part, I will always be grateful for the lessons I learnt from the WRP; whatever the conflict and disagreement its analysis was always clear. It led me to a deeper understanding of how I perceived the world; I no longer took things at face value, and I suppose it fuelled my sense of outrage at the many injustices I was becoming aware of around me.

I also grew to admire many of the Equity members who defended their principles; to stand on the stage and speak out at an Equity meeting was an exacting experience. There was always someone in the audience ready to bring you down at the first fence.

'Name!', they would thunder from the floor, as some nervous thespian stammered into speech. Or, if anyone tried to be clever and announce to the gathered assembly, 'I do not need a microphone, I am a trained actor', he or she would be shouted down with a general cry of 'Can't hear you', two lines into the speech.

It was also somewhat intimidating to know that prospective employers might be out there watching you; and judging you. That could bring trembles to the knees. So to stand up, already knowing that you were in a minority and bound to be shouted down, to my mind took enormous courage. I'm sure it was only their unshakeable belief that they were right that got them through.

I only spoke at one meeting and it was worse than any first night nerves I have ever had. I think it does go down in my own personal history as being one of the most nervous 'performances' I have ever given.

Vanessa Redgrave, of course, came in for considerable unpleasant criticism when she spoke. I remember watching in horrified silence as a resounding chant of 'Red Queen' came from a large group in the corner of the theatre. She continued calmly and persistently, her wonderful voice full of passion for her subject and, as she finished, the chant rose, but she left the stage with her dignity entirely intact. Which is more than can be said for the caterwauling and jeering crowd. I haven't always agreed politically with Vanessa, but my admiration for her was enormous. She is a woman with humanity and integrity.

I know that within me there is a bit that constantly seeks approval, which 'likes to be liked'. This can sometimes get in the way of speaking out for your beliefs. I am sure that Vanessa and others who do speak out have that same make-up in their character, but somehow they manage to overcome it. That takes a lot of courage.

I have often found myself feeling threatened by these strong minded and courageous women, feeling slightly inferior and intimidated. I have come to learn that inferiority is a problem that lies within myself, but if I am intimidated by someone, and this someone also happens to be a politician, then the fault is theirs. For surely the major thing for any politician is to be accessible to the public, whom, let's face it, they represent. It was with these feelings in mind that I set off to meet Clare Short, MP.

House of Commons chocolates and a ball point pen

MY INTEREST in Clare Short had stemmed initially from her stance on women's issues. One of the things in this society that makes me extremely angry is the lack of freedom for women to walk the streets in safety. I believe quite simply that this is one of our basic rights. That nothing seems to be done to change this situation is to me intolerable. And of course while judges continue to be lenient in the sentencing of rapists, it never will change. I am not so naive as to think that this is the only way to achieve change, but it certainly would be a step in the right direction, and would give women a feeling of hope. Now, with Clare Short installed in the Commons, I started to think that maybe somebody was batting on our side.

It was a singular experience to enter the inner sanctums of the Houses of Parliament. Like every other schoolgirl, I had 'done' the Houses of Parliament and every other 'historic place of interest' in a fast three-day visit to the capital with the school, the highlight of which was gazing out of our Paddington hotel and screaming with excitement because we believed we had spotted the Beverley Sisters in the back of a cab. My only other memory is of a visit with my family and, true to form, of me puking out of the car window all the way down the Mall. But I do have a very posed photograph of myself and my two cousins, Pauline and Marjorie, dressed alike of course, in front of 10 Downing Street. I don't remember seeing No. 10, but I do remember puking. While I lived in London, of course, the architecture became just a rather magnificent backdrop – something that was taken for granted. But now, sitting in the back of the taxi, as we swept around the building towards the visitors' entrance, I regarded it with renewed interest.

Feeling intimidated, we wound our way past the barriers to the appropriate entrance. After giving our names and intentions, we were ushered through, past wary policemen, into a lobby. Here everything changed; here tradition gave way to modern necessity. It was an odd mixture of history and a sign of the times. While in one breath you are gazing in awe at the wonders of the architecture, the security guards are gazing in amazement at the contents of your handbag. It is in situations like this that I hate myself for carrying the world and his wife around with me. And why do the most personal of my 'things' pop up into view as security fingers wrestle through the debris? And why is it that tampons that have deserted their cardboard containers look particularly obscene covered in fluff from the bottom of your bag? As bags disappear – Tesco like – down the conveyor belt, under the skirt of the X-ray machine, we were pushed into a door frame.

'What's this doing?', I practically screamed at the waiting security man.

'It's sniffing you', he answered. 'See those holes?', and

he pointed out little holes all around the doorway from top to bottom. 'They can sniff out any explosives you might be carrying, and can I have your autograph for my wife?'

On we went, down magnificent hallways and corridors, and at every doorway a policeman would greet us, ever more friendly and welcoming as we got closer to our goal.

At last we reached a 'crossroads', a beautiful round hallway with a high carved ceiling. Right at the top there were stained glass windows that would do a cathedral proud, and looking up we noticed a small section of window opening onto a clear blue sky. I found myself looking round for a window pole long enough to do the job. We gave our names and 'mission' to the man on 'reception'. A strange receptionist this, flanked by

policemen. We sat waiting for our names to be called, watching vaguely familiar faces criss-crossing in front of us; men dressed as if for a performance in a Restoration comedy in periwigs and gaiters carried messages to and fro; and parties of giggling school children were being greeted by their local MPs and then disappearing down one of the many 'rabbit warrens'.

Then at last there was Clare Short, instantly warm and welcoming. We followed her through forbidden doors, across ancient floors, glancing around us, our eyes ogling – tourists to the end. When we finally settled in a small conference room, after Clare had done battle with a 'jobsworthy' caretaker and won, we began to talk.

One thing I have learnt about politicians is that they can talk for hours with absolute clarity and charm, with seemingly absorbed interest in their subject, while their heads are thinking and assessing other things. I recognize it, because it's extremely similar to how actors operate. While you are reciting your lines, with what appears to be total commitment, the rest of your sub-conscious is assessing your audience's response, analysing your own performance and trying to remember if you switched the oven off before you came out that evening. I knew I was being 'weighed up' by Clare, but I didn't mind, rather the reverse; I would have thought her extremely naive if she had opened up her heart to me immediately, with no knowledge of my intention.

I do not at all wish to demean the content of what Clare was discussing for the history of her ride into the political arena was absorbing; it is only that I was as aware as she that we were both thinking, 'is this a person I can trust?' The only way forward, I decided, was to be totally honest about myself and my vulnerabilities, and by the end of our few hours together, and particularly when we adjourned to the bar, I believe we had found a mutual respect and liking. I certainly came away inspired, and with a feeling 'Right girls, let's get up and at 'em, there's nothing we can't do!' Until, as we were standing in the 'MPs' queue' for taxis, Margaret Thatcher swept past in the back of her chauffeur driven Jaguar, nose held high, and the thought crossed my mind, 'Some "girls" can do too much!'

We discussed Mrs T. during our meeting. I have had endless conversations with women of all age groups and political persuasions concerning Mrs Thatcher, the general consensus being that we had all as women had certain hopes when she came to power, mainly that as a wife and mother she would share feelings of humanity and experiences that are unknown to men, which would give an insight into our needs. The most moving of these conversations came out of the vulnerability of the very old, whose fears of being mugged and even raped within their own homes was beyond belief. The over-riding impression has been one of being 'let down'. Because, of course, when it comes down to it, she is in fact too far removed from ordinary women's experiences: when did she last travel on the tube, stand in the dole queue, or in a bus queue? And I know for a certainty that she doesn't stand in the taxi queue at the Commons. When did she ever panic as final demands for bills she can't pay come through the door? Will she feel those fears for her grandchild that I know many women are feeling for theirs – 'What kind of a world will be left for them to grow up in?'

My son was born in 1979, a month after she came to power. He has known no other Prime Minister. Recently he asked me if it was possible for a man to be

Prime Minister. When he is old enough to vote, what will there be left for him? What sort of education system? What sort of National Health Service? What sort of values? When he looks back at his childhood, what will he recall? Certainly not the memory I have of little bottles of school milk handed round by milk monitors, not memories of gurgling down the straw, of milk being left too long in the sun, or frozen in the snow. She 'snatched' that away in the seventies, and she has been snatching from us ever since. Perhaps her 'milk of human kindness' disappeared with the crates from the school yard.

What is so clever about Central Television's *Spitting Image* is that Fluck and Law have dressed her puppet in men's clothes, and have her smoking cigars and emulating man. This is her failing; I don't believe that she has ever brought to her position the qualities that women have. She has chosen to be a 'man' in a man's world, which no amount of 'soft voiced talking' will disguise.

What I find growing among women is a sharing and more co-operative way of life. And yet we are living at a time when the first ever woman Prime Minister stands for everything that is opposed to that sharing. It seems that she has allowed the 'men's world' to change her, instead of influencing them with 'female' values. This has led me to believe that a few token women holding prominent positions in society is not enough.

It was encouraging to hear from Clare Short that there now seems to be a shift in the new generation of women politicians. In the past women had to make it like men, they had to talk about industry and transport and so on. They never really dared to discuss children, rape, contraception and cervical cancer because there was an unspoken feeling that people would turn round and say, 'Huh, you're a woman, you're not a proper politician'. But now they talk about everything and women can bring their own experiences to these debates, especially to transport, because women use public transport more than anyone else. Even in car owning families the man usually takes the car away.

It was the bringing of 'female' qualities to politics, and standing up to your own beliefs, that I wanted to pursue with Clare Short. I wanted to know how hard it was to operate within that extremely male dominated building, where a male majority is making decisions that give us and our children the chances of a reasonable life, or a decidedly second rate one. Remembering my experiences at Equity meetings, and that terror of facing a hostile audience, I asked how she felt about getting up to speak in Parliament, that most hostile of audiences.

'I had a sense that what I had to do was stand up for all the things I believed in, even if I got things thrown at me. I think there are a lot of people out there, sometimes you have to be brave and just do it. The tragedy for me politically is that I thought that me moving into politics was about expanding the kind of luck and chances I've had to everyone. I really thought it was an inevitable process. But I've lived through this period when it has all shrunk and torn apart, and yet it seems to me that something is going on amongst women.'

She fished around in her handbag and brought out some of the letters that she had just received; they were from women expressing gratitude that she was there speaking for them.

'I have learned from these letters that women *do* see me as there for them. So when I'm feeling lousy, and thinking, "I'm hardly having any effect, and maybe I should go and do another job", then I think of their support and tell myself, you don't have to be brave. Just do it. Well, sometimes you have to be brave!'

Clare Short has been an MP since 1983. I felt that all those years of 'speaking out' must have given her a certain amount of confidence:

'It's a continuing journey. I can remember being at Labour Party meetings, when I was scared to ask questions from the back. And now I can quite happily speak to a few hundred people. But there'll always be this next thing coming along that makes you scared.'

I know exactly what she means; I've often felt as I faced another challenge, 'Where did it go – all that confidence I had yesterday?' But I know that it's taking risks and facing challenges that in the end make you grow. For Clare Short, though, it doesn't get any easier; it's almost like 'The more you know, the harder it gets.'

Clare went on: 'The thing is not to be frightened. It's partly to do with being a woman, because you are so unusual when you're here. You continue to be unusual. You don't get sucked in. You have your sense of difference. Even in what you wear.'

I had noticed this. Any MPs I've ever set eyes on always seem to look the same; they have their expensive suits and shirts, and the only way you can tell them apart is from the colour of their ties! They all look as if they've got a uniform on. Clare agreed.

'But we come along and, because we're not supposed to be here, there isn't a uniform for us, so we can wear what we like: suits, or trousers, long skirts or short skirts. Sometimes I think "I'll be respectable today", or sometimes I'll be a bit mischievous and put on something not quite right for this place. I love that.'

So what for the future? I remember talking to the

miners' wives who, despite what they have been through, have come out of it still optimistic. This optimism burned through when Sylvia, one of the miners' wives, said:

'There'll be a revolution, and it will be the women. It's the only thing that I've got to believe in. It's got to happen; it's the women of the world that will do it. After our experience we haven't completely gone back to the sink.'

Clare Short echoed this.

'Despite these bad times, I feel this real hopefulness about women: all ages, all ethnic backgrounds, all class backgrounds. It's going on all over the world, this sort of movement amongst women, wanting some more space and respect for themselves.'

I think it is important to stress at this point that it isn't just a case of all women are 'lovely' and all men are 'bad'. But there is something in the way that girls are brought up, and in the things that are expected of them, that brings out certain human characteristics such as honesty about emotion, humanity, warmth and a certain amount of selflessness. Values which I recognize and hope to bring out in my son, but with the full knowledge that, as he grows up and is influenced by the outside world, this will be no easy task. Clare Short seized on this:

'The fact that it is hard is part of it', she said. 'I think people just climbing the ladder in politics, or any other walk of life, are less complete without some of the pain – the messy times we've all been through. If you can hold on to them, and admit they happened, not pretend they didn't, then that in itself makes us bigger.'

At the end of our chat we adjourned to the bar, wandering back down venerable corridors. In the old Westminster Hall I stood on the marked stone where

Charles the First had received his death sentence and looked at the spot where Winston Churchill had lain in state. The whole place was steeped in such history and tradition it was hard to keep a hold on reality. Inside the bar I felt really close to the 'action'. A debate was in full flood, bells were ringing and everywhere there was a sense of activity. Television monitors were placed at convenient points – one in every bar, of course, to keep the members up to date. I had the feeling of being on a film set, and when I glanced across the room and spotted a well-known face, I exclaimed in excitement, 'Look, look, there's the actor who plays Cecil Parkinson!'

Male MPs from all sides nodded continually in Clare's direction. Suddenly I saw the reversal in role: she *is* different; she is attractive and sexy, she hasn't joined 'the club' and become a 'man'. Her very difference makes them seek her approval, and respect her.

On the way out I nipped into their souvenir shop and bought my House of Commons chocolates and a ball point pen.

17 97 ways to cook baked beans: the miners' wives

THERE ARE things in our lives that 'touch' us and move us into activity. Seeing other people's plight moves us out of our armchairs. When something touches us personally, we leave those armchairs and life will never be the same again.

On 5 March 1984 the Yorkshire miners came out on strike in protest at the proposed closure of Cortonwood Colliery, setting off a national miners' strike. They went back on 3 March the following year.

I have always had great sympathy for the miners. During the period I was at Coventry we did a play about the coal mining industry. We were taken to the mines at Corley, Warwickshire, where a trip 'down below' was organized. It was a hell hole. The history of coal mining, the conditions and struggles of the mining communities, I always see now in the light of that glimpse of the reality and hardship of their world.

The strike was hard; of that there is no question. So what happened during it, when these families left their armchairs? It seemed to me that the women's role in this strike was more prominent than in any other mining strike. When I talk to the women who went through it, it reminds me of talking to women who went through the war. They found a sense of purpose, a fulfilment they had never experienced before.

It was to learn about that experience that I arranged to meet some women who had lived through the strike. I was feeling a little nervous for I had no idea what to expect. Like everyone else I had been subjected to the media coverage of the strike, and for a moment it flashed through my mind that I might be about to launch into a meeting with a group of extremely bitter women, 'hardened lefties' who would fill me with 'dogma' and send me on my way.

As I was making a bad job of parking my car, the door opened and Sylvia, our hostess, came down the path to greet me. She seemed slightly shy as she ushered me into her sitting room, where the dog was lying in front of the fire. I was introduced to her husband, Ken, a big and cheerful miner who was dispatched to open the bottle of wine I had brought with me to relax us all. Joyce was sitting in the corner of the sofa and greeted me with a huge smile. We immediately struck up a conversation, which was interesting but at that point steering well away from the miners' strike. Then there was a ring on the door bell, and what appeared to be a never ending stream of women walked in. When I had stopped panicking I realized that there were only three of them. Madge, beautifully made up and well groomed, came and sat beside me. Irene, older than the others, removed herself to a corner of the room by the fire and regarded me quizzically over her glasses. She took out a notebook and pen and placed them in readiness on the arm of the chair. And last, but by no means least, was Dot, who gave me a cheerful smile and plonked herself down by Sylvia's chair. They regarded me, and I regarded them. Suddenly I knew it would be okay; and it was. These women weren't 'hardened fanatics'; they were the sort of women I had grown up with, who had lived around me all my life: northern women, mums, warm and full of fun and care. And until the strike came along, they were leading what they would call 'ordinary lives'.

But the strike had come and it had changed them.

Sylvia is an attractive blonde woman, full of vitality. She has been married twice, first to Bill, who died leaving her with three children, two boys and a girl, and then to Ken, a miner. Bill had been a Ford worker so she had grown used to strikes; her married life with him had seemed to be full of them. She was never involved, she was at home with her babies. The only thing she ever got involved in was the PTA at school. Sylvia describes her life in those pre-1984 years as 'fairly mundane and ordinary'. But by all accounts it was a good life and they were a happy family. She was a canteen lady at the pit when the strike started. She recalls:

'I worked into the strike. My husband Ken worked at the pit and so did my two sons. And they were amongst the first to stand at the top of the lane. My sister, who worked with me at the pit, and I kept saying, "We should be with them", but I kept crossing the picket line. Our union kept saying that we should stay in the canteen because in those early days the men were allowed in from the picket lines for their breakfast. But every morning I would get up and I could hear those picket lines, and I used to have to go through, and past my husband and my two sons. Some mornings I just couldn't do it, and I'd just go home. Then work would

ring and say I had to go in. I felt like the advert on the
tele, with the cows moving backwards and forwards.'

So I asked her, 'What was it then, that finally made
you come out?'

'I wanted to come out all the time; I knew deep down
that that was where I should be. But there were four of
us here at home, my daughter had just left school, and
Billy, my eldest son, was married with a small baby and
another one on the way. I was giving him a bit of money,
and still paying the rent and trying to keep us going.
Really, I was justifying myself. I was terrified.'

Before she could continue the door bell rang; she
crossed the room and opened the door to her young son
and his girlfriend, who took one look into the room and
disappeared into the kitchen. Settling herself down
again, she went on:

'Some days my sister and I would have our coats on,
ready to go home, then they'd say in the canteen, "Don't,
you're better off here, you're helping them here". It was
terrible. So one day Ken said, "That's it, I'm going to
turn you back today. I'll turn you back." And it was the
biggest relief in my life when I turned back and didn't
cross the picket line.'

As the strike wore on Sylvia realized that to stand on
the picket line was not enough; there was a growing
hardship around her. With the other women she helped
set up a social centre, and from there they could operate
the soup kitchens. It was also a place where the wives
could come and talk, and seek help; a lot of the women at
home didn't really understand what was going on.

'I understood the women's point of view', Sylvia
explained. 'When a woman's at home with the kids, and
doesn't know what's going on, only what she reads in
the newspaper, or what she sees on the television, then I

understand her feelings; my own daughter-in-law was at home with a small baby. You've got wages coming in every week and you're paying the bills. Then suddenly you've got nothing. And you've got babies to see to.'

'So how did you make them understand?', I asked her.

'We brought the women to the centre, or we went out to talk to them. We tried to explain because their husbands weren't going home and telling them. They were just going home and keeping them out of it, like "it's nothing to do with you". In fact, that was exactly how I'd been treated. You know – although you're not getting any money, it's nothing to do with you!

'My daughter-in-law became one of the best we've ever had at the centre. At the beginning she used to say "What's going on? Suddenly I've got to say to my little lad, no more ice creams when he's always had them." But coming to the centre and getting involved, she grew to understand.'

Leaning forward she finished with excitement:

'I think a lot of the women became aware of what was going on, a lot were young married women. We set up the soup kitchens; we went out speaking; we went out collecting. We had to learn very fast. I don't think it will be useless what we learnt, I think it was a real education. I feel my life only started when I came out on strike.'

I turned to Madge, sitting on my left on the settee, and asked her how it had affected her life.

'I'd had a pretty full life. When I had my little girl I suffered from after effects. It used to drive me daft in the house, so I got involved in the church. I became a Sunday school teacher and I joined the Mothers' Union. I started to run a playgroup. So my life was completely taken up. We had already gone through the 1972 strike when my little girl was about two. It was all over very quick and you didn't feel the effects too much. It was perhaps as well. We'd been buying our house and we'd the mortgage to pay. We used to get these food coupons from different shops. I used to go and spend them. The family helped so we got over that period and the children grew up. And then the big strike came. Apart from doing what I normally did, which was Sunday school, Mothers' Union, and the playgroup, I became actively involved in the miners' strike.

'My husband had worked in the pit for thirty years, he was on the executive. I found it hard to adjust to it, but I found I could fit it in. I used to go to different meetings, speaking. It was emotional to me. I was never politicized. I had never thought of the police as an enemy, but I did do on the strike. I couldn't understand people disbelieving what I told them. I said, "My phone's tapped" and they laughed, "Oh, you're imagining it!" But it was. Isn't that terrible. But it was true. It was then I became politicized.'

She shook her head, and said thoughtfully,

'I couldn't understand anyone not looking at it from our point of view. But I've come to the conclusion that people don't want to know. They'll let it ride over their heads, and it's not until it hits them that they become aware. That's too late then. It's shutting the stable door when the horse has bolted.

'We got a copy of the Ridley Report, and we tried to spell it out to the people. We were on strike not only for us, but for the whole country. We were trying to save jobs, our jobs and everybody's, but they wouldn't believe. The Ridley Report said "Get rid of the big unions and the smaller ones will be easy". If you remember, during the strike, the railway workers, the dock workers and the shipyard workers all threatened to come out but they paid them off. "Pay them off whatever it costs".'

The final report of the Conservative Party policy group on nationalized industries was drafted by the Conservative MP, Nicholas Ridley, in 1978. It was published by *The Economist* on 27 May of that year. The article read:

> In an annexe to this report, Mr Ridley and some of his co-authors have been pondering how to counter any 'political threat' from those they regard as 'the enemies of the next Tory government'. They believe that in the first or second year after the Tories' election, there might be a major challenge from a trade union either over a wage claim or over redundancies.

The Economist went on to outline the Conservative strategy for countering this 'threat':

> The Group believes that the most likely battle-ground will be the coal industry. They would like a Thatcher government to:
> (a) Build up maximum coal stocks, particularly at the power stations;
> (b) Make contingency plans for the import of coal;
> (c) Encourage the recruitment of non-union lorry drivers by haulage companies to help move coal where necessary;
> (d) Introduce dual coal/oil firing in all power stations as quickly as possible.
> The Group believes that the greatest deterrent to any strike would be 'to cut off the money supply to the strikers, and make the union finance them'.

There should be a large, mobile squad of police equipped and prepared to uphold the law against violent picketing. 'Good non-union drivers' should be recruited to cross picket lines with police protection.

Madge confirmed bitterly:

'And that's what they did with us. They said we were defeated, but we weren't. Not morally. We went back together, not in dribs and drabs. Everyone said we were defeated, but personally I know we weren't.'

Throughout my conversation with Madge, Irene had continued to regard me, rather like a headmistress regards a pupil. Every now and then she would take up a pencil and write a few notes. Now she looked at me hard and said,

'Who did you say you were, Sue Lawley?' The others screamed with laughter, and she smiled. 'Well, I don't know do I. I don't watch television.

'I'm older than Sylvia and the rest; I'm sixty-four. I come from a mining family, grandfather and father, so I knew as a child what the 1926 strike and the thirties were like. I also knew about the struggle, apart from the miners, what the people went through. The Salvation Army feeding the children, and the means test. The same thing is beginning to happen today. So all this was in the back of my mind, imprinted on my mind.' She spoke quietly and with passion and the others listened respectfully.

'I became a nurse, I married in 1948, and I married into a family with no miners at all. My son went into the pit in 1979. When the strike came, me being Labour of course, I said to my son, "You don't go to work. We'll have no scabs in this family." I knew this from a child. I knew everything we had gone through. Lady Astor had

called us "earthworms in the earth". We were nothing;
we were kept down. I used to be called "Mrs Red"
because I spoke this way. My son has turned out to be
like me in his views, only stronger, more political. He
had three months in jail for stopping scabs, which was
very sad. I would find wholeheartedly for the miners
even if I hadn't come from a mining family. I would have
still felt the same because of what we went through in
the thirties.'

We were silent when Irene finished speaking; reflec-
tive. Then Joyce began to tell her story:

'I come from a mining family too; my mother and
father both worked at the pit. My husband worked there
as well, but my life was completely turned over by the
strike. I have three children, well one's my grandchild,
but I've had her since she was born. I was always at
church. I was the secretary of the Women's Fellowship
there, but when the strike came I completely changed.
The night the Women's Fellowship was on at the church
was the night we met for our women's group at the
colliery. So the church side went.'

I said I thought this must have been a difficult
decision. She nodded.

'I did think about it. I had a talk to our minister, he
comes from Bradford. He comes from a mining place
himself. I said to him that I didn't know what I was
doing: ". . . my mind's there at the pit, and yet I know I'm
the secretary here". But I was thinking to myself that I
was better off at the pit. And he replied, "Well, I can
understand your feelings, and I feel the same as you.
You can do more good going there than you can here." So
my life was completely changed. I still go to church, but
I don't go to the Women's Fellowship because I broke
away.'

There seemed to be a pattern in all that they were saying, a massive involvement demanding all their time and energy. Joyce agreed.

'For us, for the women involved in the strike, it was nearly twenty-four hours a day, every day. I worked as well, but I was up at five o'clock in the morning, and on the picket line. We'd come off the picket line at about eight am, go home, get ready, and be off to work. Come home from work, the phone would ring, "Would you go to such and such a place tonight and speak there?" I would first have me tea, see the children were all right, and off I'd go. Probably till midnight. You couldn't just say, "Well, I'll have a night off tonight", because if you was involved, you was involved. You'd just pack your bags and go for days to different places. Collecting and things, you know. My life was changed altogether.

'I mean our family's always been political. I don't mean in the sense of going to meetings or anything like that. But I'm speaking out at work, and following the television, and if there's elections or anything, I'm up all night; we all are. But now they tell me I'm a militant. I just don't take any notice of them. I have a mind of my own, you see. My husband didn't want me to get involved, but I don't care what he says, I have my own mind and I do what I want.' She shrugged.

'It's funny you know, I never used to go outside the door. The only time I went outside the door was to go to church.'

Although there was no question of the demands made on their time, the overall feeling for me was that, hard as it was, they had enjoyed it; they seemed to be fulfilled. Dot practically leapt to her feet.

'Yes, yes!', she exclaimed, 'I am a mother with four kids and a job. I wasn't involved in anything like the strike. Nothing political. I've got a very political and unionized husband. I went through the 1972 strike, but I didn't get involved. I didn't have time to get involved. Mainly though, he didn't tell me much about it.

'But *this* strike was different. It was *exciting*. You know yourself when you get on stage and your adrenalin starts going. That's how we were. When I worked, I would get to rock bottom. Only during the strike I used to come home from work and say, "Right, there's a meeting tonight", and in half-an-hour I was wide awake. It was great. We were nervous when we got there though.

'We had a miners' wives group. It was two or three in the morning before I was getting home. Then up again at seven, to work, then back to another meeting. Great. The people you met. Ooooh, it was exciting! I mean the things you learn! 97 ways to cook baked beans!'

I was reminded of what Clare Short had said about holding on to the hard times and the 'messy times' and not pretending that they didn't happen, because it's those very messy bits that make you grow. I could see how these women had grown, how this experience had 'touched' them, and how they would never be the same again. I turned to Dot:

'Dot', I asked her musingly, 'What are the other 96 ways to cook baked beans?'

Match of the day

FROM THE AGE of six years my father used to take me with him to watch the match on a Saturday afternoon. I've always thought his loyalties must invariably have been split, for he was both a Liverpool Football Club supporter and a St Helens Rugby League supporter. But the latter was closer to home. My Grandfather Wright, my Dad's father, was also an avid fan, and sometimes we all went together. And at eighty-six years of age one Saturday, he watched a match, walked the three miles home, and three days later passed away peacefully in his sleep. Like my Dad and my Grandad, I loved football. And by the time I was fourteen I had descended from my Dad's shoulders to stand on the terraces without parental guidance.

By the late fifties there was nothing you could tell me or my friend Marje about our team, even down to the size of the prop forward's thighs. We followed the 'Saints' loyally and steadfastly until, in pursuit of my theatrical career, I left home for London and was forced to abandon them.

The south hadn't embraced the delights of Rugby League, and even watching the All-Blacks play Wales couldn't recompense my loss. So the Saturday event was, for a while, shelved. It was a few years later, while I was working at the Cockpit Theatre, that my interest was rekindled. Opposite the theatre was the local pub and many of its regulars were Arsenal supporters. It was a party of these 'locals' who persuaded me one afternoon to visit Highbury and watch their team. I did just that. And, difficult as some of you may find it to believe, Arsenal were good to watch. I believed that I had found a replacement for my beloved Saints. That was until Arsenal played Liverpool.

I can't remember whether it was the quality of the play, the attractiveness of the players or being surrounded again by Liverpool accents and wit. Maybe it was the combination of all three, but I know that Arsenal were immediately relegated and, from then on, whenever Liverpool played in London, I'd be there with the Kop, rejoicing in the camaraderie.

I remember going to watch them play at Tottenham. I took my friend John with me, a theatre designer and fellow Liverpudlian, with no previous experience of football supporting. We were only a few minutes into the game when the referee was injured; one of the linesmen quickly took his place, but we were left with a linesman short. And it seemed they weren't carrying a spare. A few minutes later there was an announcement on the loud speaker requesting any professional referee in the crowd to make himself known so they could continue the game. Comments resounded around the pitch, some humorous, others not so. Suddenly a great roar went up and thousands of Liverpool voices sang as one:

'He's here, he's there, he's every f*****g where!' And Jimmy Hill in his natty black shorts and waving his flag took up his position on the line, and play recommenced. My friend was stunned.

'How did they know?', he marvelled. 'How did they all know the words? And when to start singing?' For the crowd's response was so immediate you would have thought they had been rehearsing for weeks. I've never been able to work it out myself. And the Kop's chorusing still remains for me one of the seven wonders of the world.

As I have grown older, my support for the club has been total, but my visits less frequent. It's not the game I've deserted, but rather the travelling to and from the ground, and the feeling of vulnerability in a crowd. It's sad, because I would have liked nothing better than to share my love of football with my small son, but as things stand at the moment there is no way I would put him at risk.

About four years ago I had a special treat: Liverpool were to play Manchester United in the Milk Cup Final at Wembley, and Craig Johnston, then Liverpool's number ten, had presented me with two tickets. They were delivered to work on the Friday before the game and, as soon as they were actually in my possession, I rang my Dad:

'Pack your sandwiches, Dad', I said, 'we're off to Wembley in the morning.'

There had been a weekend when I was small when my mother and father were going to Wembley for a Cup Final. They had planned to stay all weekend and see a show. I can't honestly remember now if I was genuinely ill or just faking, but I know I cried a lot at the thought of being left. So they didn't go. It was only when I looked down from my bedroom window and saw my Dad sitting in his greenhouse, his head in his hands, that I realized how great his disappointment was, and how selfish I had been. I hoped in some way that this trip to Wembley might compensate for that lost weekend many years before.

It was a day certainly that I'll never forget. We travelled in style, first class rail tickets to London, and then on to football specials to Wembley. There's nothing that can equal the atmosphere of a Cup Final. It's always wonderful to relive that feeling, when you are finally through the barriers, have found your way through the maze, and climbed the stairs. You stand at the top and see the crowd beneath you, and the green turf; and feel the excitement.

We had never had seats like these before. We'd never had seats before. There we were, smack bang in the middle with a view that you would kill for. Because I had never been in that position I was able to observe the crowd more than I had when I had stood at one end amongst them.

It was tribal. No question, that's what it was. Manchester United's fans at their end sang their songs, chanted their chants and, then with a great roar, up came their colours and proudly they presented them and laid their banners down. The Kop raised theirs and in turn roared out *their* chants, and with rising emotion the strains of 'You'll never walk alone' drowned out the opposition. We were all ready for battle to commence.

It was a great game; at half-time, as my Dad and I sat eating our sandwiches, lovingly prepared by my Mum ('You'll get nothing there'), a man wended his way through the crowd and, with an outstretched hand, greeted my father. The man had been his replacement when he retired. And somehow in the midst of all those people he had spotted my Dad and, reunited, they talked of the old days. We decided we would leave the ground before the end of the match but, as we were leaving Manchester United equalized, and extra time had to be played. So we stayed and stayed, then rushed for a cab. It had been a triumph with Liverpool the worthy winners.

A train was just leaving as we reached Euston, and we jumped aboard. As we settled down, we looked around at our fellow travellers. My Dad had plonked himself down next to none other than Tom Finney. He was a great player of my Dad's generation and had, like my father, been a plumber. They talked plumbing and football and were bathed in nostalgia all the way home. My Dad's day was complete. I was glad to have shared it with him. The following year it was Liverpool and Everton's turn to fight for the Milk Cup. Again I had tickets, but my Dad bowed out:

'I'll go out on that memory', he said. 'There's nothing could equal that.'

On a beautiful spring morning one Saturday in April, I was working outside in the garden, struggling to write this book but being constantly distracted with the desire just to sit and feel this first warm sun of the year on my face. I continued on and off like this for the next few hours. Then another distraction began to creep into my mind. Liverpool would have kicked off by now in the semi-final cup tie with Notts Forest. I had been offered tickets for the game, but the niggling fear that I was getting too far behind had kept me at home.

I wandered into the kitchen and switched on the television. As the picture came into view I stood looking at it in a bemused kind of way, not quite understanding what I was seeing. The players were on the field half playing, glancing around at the ever increasing number of fans on the pitch. Some of the players seemed to have stopped altogether, and were being berated by excited fans who came on pointing back towards the terraces where, from behind the cages, other fans were screaming out, desperately trying to communicate with the police. Some fans were being hauled up to the stands above. I went cold; memories of Bradford and Heysel stole into my mind, and I stood rooted to the spot, gawping in hypnotized horror as I had when those two previous tragedies unfolded. A policeman ran across the pitch, the match was stopped. The players left the field. From then on the enormity of what we were witnessing began to unfold. And as the toll of the dead rose, we could only watch in stunned disbelief. Ninety-five people on that beautiful spring day had set out to watch a game of football and would not be going home.

That Sunday evening I went with my cousin Stewart to the Catholic cathedral. He had witnessed Heysel and Hillsborough, and was deeply upset. We walked along with everyone else in silence through the city, and though we had arrived in good time, the cathedral was already packed. We stood with thousands of others outside that massive monument. The police opened the great glass doors so that we could hear, and a priest held his portable radio with Radio City's transmission of the service high in the air. And together, alongside Everton supporters, we sang 'Abide with me' and the Twenty-third Psalm, and we cried and prayed. Men and women wept openly and three men brought their dead friend's scarf and it was passed in silence through the crowd, into the cathedral where they wanted it to lie. Then as silently as we had all gathered, we left.

It was uncanny, the stillness in the city over those next few days. To visit Anfield was harrowing yet restorative. Again we stood in hushed queues and read the simple poems and dedications. We marvelled at the flowers and the souvenirs which must have meant such sacrifices to grieving fans. The sight of groups of young men clutching their bunches of flowers with tears pouring down their faces was almost too much to bear.

So many funerals; so many tributes; so many minutes' silence. And through it all the lament of the bitter sweet anthem, 'You'll never walk alone'.

And so the city grieved with the bereaved, and in particular the players and their wives. And because of their selflessness and understanding the team will always represent far more to the people of Liverpool than just another football team.

I went to the Cup Final and it was a magnificent display of Merseyside united; that Liverpool won the Cup was a fitting tribute.

 *The good enough
mother*

ONE THING no one can ever prepare any woman for is
the overwhelming love you feel for your child. I can't
honestly say that in my case it happened at the precise
moment my baby was born. I was too exhausted and my
muscles developed such a severe attack of shaking that
they had to bring me a cup of very sweet tea, which they
had to transfer to a baby's feeder cup. For a moment *I*
was the baby.

My senses were taking everything else in, as indeed
they had through the whole of the labour: the cherry
blossom in full bloom, outside the delivery room; the
midwife's joy as if it was the only baby she'd ever
delivered and my very explicit language at the final
stage. But I was I suppose so much into my own feelings
at that time that it was difficult to know what I felt for
the child. I was stunned; I think it took me a day to
realize what had happened. I was overwhelmingly
moved by the experience, I wanted immediately to be in
contact with other women who had had children. It was
like a secret we could share; when I heard of women who
had been in the classes with me going through a hard
labour I wanted to weep and go and hold them. I'd never
considered myself a great feminist, but I had such a

deep feeling of wanting to share with and support other women. It brought me closer to my women friends, and this feeling has never left me. It was a precious experience and I am so glad that I had it. But then came the fear. This love was so terrifying, because I might lose him; I felt so inadequate with this little mite. I thought I might drop him or damage him, I didn't know how to look after him. I couldn't bear the responsibility. I looked with such admiration at two teenage girls on the ward, dangling their first borns from their hips. I pointed this out to a midwife.

'It's because you're older, love, you know the dangers.'

To say I was inadequate is an understatement. The major trauma in my life at that time was my inability to bath this day-old infant. We had had a demonstration on 'bathing the baby'. We'd all sat with our huge stomachs (which we all thought would have disappeared the moment the baby was born) all traumatized with the experience and watched the nurse bath this wonderfully behaved 'infant Meryl Streep'. Nothing to it, I thought, and went back to bath mine. I dutifully filled the bowl with water, tested the temperature with my elbow, soaped the little naked screaming child all over, and tried to get my fingers in the right position to dangle the slithering object into the water. My child was now yelling with full force in the most evil way. I couldn't hold him, he was turning puce, I abandoned the project and burst into tears. I was a failure. The midwife finished the job for me and I wondered what would happen when I left hospital. The dirtiest baby in the world would be mine.

The next day the midwife and I bathed a Ribena bottle. It went very well. The actual baby bathing that followed seemed to be going very well too – fingers in the right position, baby screaming but well soaped (I was trying not to notice the screaming). Everything was perfect, except that I had forgotten the one thing that mattered; I hadn't put any water in the bowl. Tears of shame and humiliation as the midwife once again took control. Of course, eventually common sense takes over, I discovered squeezy bath soap, I breast fed him a little, to take his hunger pains away, which stopped him screaming. I found my own way through the struggle. Bathtimes became a joy and not a time for a nervous breakdown. I never really understood why it had to be so complicated, so hard learned. It's such a delicate time in your life. The tears are always so near.

When I came out of hospital my paranoia increased. The baby was born in a very hot June, and inside the hospital we baked in an even temperature of eighty

degrees. So when I came home on went the central heating. The baby was ensconced in the pram dressed in practically all the clothes he possessed and covered with all available blankets.

'Don't smoke!', I'd scream at my friends, 'let those cats out! Where are the dogs?' Everything normal became menacing. My friends threatened to leave me and the baby broke out in a rash. I searched in the books for symptoms – it seemed to me he could have anything from German measles to rabies. I rang my retired midwife friend, Molly.

'He's got a rash,' I wailed.

'Darling', she soothed, 'no baby ever died of a rash. How many covers has he got on him? How many clothes?'

I told her.

'How hot is he?' I was silent. Quietly she said, 'I think you'll probably find it's a heat rash'. She was so wonderfully practical – so reassuring. The clothes and covers came off, my friends didn't desert me, although the cats did. And my dogs were like sentinels either side of the pram, guarding their new property with obvious pride.

What did I learn from all this, from those days when I wept into the nappies at the sink, and every night when I woke up in cold sweats in case I had lost this loved one? And, yes, I did wake him to see if he was still breathing. I learned that I was a grown-up, that I was responsible for another life, that my love was huge, but would never be huge enough. And that I was very frightened. It was really the beginning for me of whether or not I could ever be a 'good enough mother'.

All of us mothers of course have our pregnancy and birth stories, some of them good, some of them not so, and we do like to talk about it; to share it.

When I played a birth scene on *Brookside* some years ago, it became a responsibility to get it right. After all, a large percentage of our audience had had their own experience, and I could imagine them at home, commenting.

'Oh no, I'm sorry, but that's not right. I didn't do that. She's not got it right at all.' Or worse, 'I don't believe that.' Then of course there were all the pregnant women who had yet to face it. I didn't want to be sweating, heaving and moaning, and sending them into a real panic. I just decided that all I could do was copy my own son's birth. I knew the truth of that. The day after it was shown, we'd sat in the canteen at work chatting, and I realized it had opened the door for people to talk about their own child's birth. One of our joiners talked vividly of how moving the birth of his twin sons had been. To be there, to see it. And my own mother, for the first time, talked of my birth and how similar it was to what she had seen me portray.

'Oh, all those little pantings you were doing', she said, 'it took me right back.'

Occasionally, of course, it's *not* joyous. We all carry different memories.

'It's funny the things that stick in your mind', my friend, Edie McCardle, said about the birth of her son, John. 'I had been told I could have gas and air', she went on, 'but it was being used by another woman.' Edie, only twenty-one at the time, was having her first child, and pleading with the nurse for some relief.

'*Please* could I have the gas and air?', she repeatedly asked. But it never came. When the pain became intolerable the nurse had said to her:

'Put your arms around me tight.'

Edie said, ' "Do what?" I was only skinny then,' she

continued, 'but I got hold of her and I held her really tight, and she went, "Get off!" and she hit me right across the face. I couldn't let go of her, you see. The *pain*. And she went Bang! It sent all the breath out of my body.' She also remembers that immediately after her delivery they brought her her breakfast. She recalls:

'They brought me a kipper and cornflakes. It was eight o'clock and breakfast time. John was born at ten to. They put the kipper on a steel locker by the bed, the kipper on top, and the cornflakes below. And the kipper fell in the cornflakes. It's funny the things that stick in your mind.'

Eventually we recover from the birth, we adapt ourselves to motherhood and then, as they grow, we develop other fears. Fears for their safety, fears for their health, and sometime just the plain fear of not being able to bring them up as a happy and well adjusted adult, male or female.

It is not unusual in my house to start the day in a frenzy. Small boy's pyjamas hit the deck, to be scooped up into the huge mouth of our retriever, and carried off to distant corners of house or garden and unceremoniously dumped.

'Where's my clothes?', demands small boy.

'Where you left them,' retorts demented Mum.

Ten minutes to nine and no sign of small boy.

'Where are you? Have you cleaned your teeth? Washed your face, combed your hair?' No reply.

Demented mother rushes into bedroom to discover small child wearing only underpants and one sock, lying on the floor, reading. Lost to the world with *Asterix in Corsica*. Without concern he regards me.

'I can't find my clothes', he yawns.

'If you put them away when you took them off . . .' And

I am away round the home, 'retrieving' bits of school uniform.

Reflecting on all this one day, I began to realize that I was not only making a rod for my own back, but one for some unfortunate woman or women who might eventually share their life with my son. Half the time I run about clearing up my son's mess because it's actually quicker to do it myself. But how much of it is fulfilling my own sense of being needed, of being the 'little mother'? I had mistakenly believed that my son was quite liberated. I taught him to cook, and ironing was to be next. Then I heard some friends discussing their husbands' liberalization.

'My husband's very liberated', said one, 'he always does the cooking.'

'He probably likes it', responded the other caustically. Then I recalled a conversation with Mavis Nicholson. She had never minded ironing for her kids, she told me, but when one day they started dictating to her how they wanted their clothes pressed, she'd informed them:

'I'll do basic ironing – but if it's "precision ironing" you're after then you can do it yourself.'

A lot of people say, and I have to admit that I agree with them, that it's the way you bring up your sons that makes them what they are. What a responsibility.

Recently I've had long discussions with my son about his contribution to household duties, with the intention of giving him some idea of what's behind the 'running of a home', so that as he grows, he will have an independence, and an ability to stand on his own feet. If he had been a girl I would have done exactly the same. I didn't want my son to grow up as some men have, believing, as Judy Spiers told me her brothers did, that toilet rolls grow in the bathroom.

However, I feel rather a hypocrite when I chastize Joel about the state of his room. I'm not a very tidy person myself and I know that, as a child, I was positively 'slut-like'. When I was recently bemoaning the state of Joel's 'boudoir' my mother reminded me of mine when I was his age, and of how in desperation one day she had pushed open my door and wheeled in the hoover. Three days later the hoover had not been returned, so she ventured forth to find it. There it was where she had left it, festooned with coats and hats and buried in the debris like all other available 'bits of furniture'.

It was interesting one day when Joel, sick of either my continual demands or of his friend's reactions – 'Oooh Joel, this is a *mess!*' – decided to do something about it. It took rather a long time. As old toys lost for months beneath stale clothes and sweet wrappers were uncovered he then had to re-enjoy them, or re-read long lost books. But when he had finished, what pride, what achievement. And although it would not have gained many points on the Richter scale, it certainly wasn't a bad job done. Because *he* had slaved over it, it stayed that way for longer; at least three days. Then the norm was re-established. An important lesson had been learned; by me of course. That sense of achievement was my clue. I had to continue on that line and, even if it takes forever, we will get there in the end. Actually, if I'm honest, his sense of achievement in anything he does is more important to me than a tidy room. I believe it's vital that he should know how much I love him; I think it's so soul destroying for any child to be put down by a parent. They must have their sense of worth, they must value themselves. That's the job I want to do for Joel. I hope I can be a good enough parent to succeed.

Again I seek reassurance from other women, learning from their experience. There are so many things I want for my son. I want him to be self reliant and independent; loving and kind; to be himself and go free. I don't want to put all my failings and aspirations on his shoulders. My friend May Thomson told me of an old north American Indian poem long forgotten by her except for the line:

The child is an arrow from the bow. You let them go. You let them go free.

20 *Taxi*

WHEN I WAS a drama student, the principal taught me a very important lesson. He said that 'you carry things on the stage with you'. He didn't just mean props, but rather your own character and often your own character failings. If they aren't the same traits as the character you are playing, you are in dead lumber. I'll give you an example. The principal said,

'Sue, you tend to walk into a room and apologize for your presence, before you even open your mouth'. Now apparently that's exactly what I did when I went on stage. My body language would say:

'Sorry everyone, sorry that I'm here on this stage. Sorry you've got to look at this nonentity reciting its lines.' Naturally, if you are playing a part like Lady Macbeth, this behaviour is not going to get you very far. Now I understand all this in relation to acting. Technique and stage craft have taught me to get rid of, in the main, my own personal hang-ups on stage. But so far I have not succeeded in transferring this achievement to real life.

Believe me I do try and put all that I have learned into practice. But somehow I always seem to let myself down. Let me tell you something that happened to me recently. I had been working in London for a couple of weeks, on this book as a matter of fact, which had involved quite a lot of travelling by taxi – from place of work to friends' houses: same route, same time and, approximately, give or take a few pence, the same price. One particular evening, homeward bound and day dreaming as usual in the back of the cab, I glanced out of the window and had no recollection of where I was. I looked at the meter; the fare was saying that I should, by rights, be nearly home. But where was I?

'West Drayton', the cabbie replied gruffly in response to my question. I hadn't the least idea where West Drayton was, but I knew it was nowhere near where I should be.

'It's taking rather a long time, this journey', I spluttered bravely.

'On the contrary', he returned, 'I thought we were making excellent time.' The next few miles or rather the next few pounds continued in silence. But tension was in the air. My eyes were glued to the clock as the money mounted up. I felt a mixture of anger and fear at what was happening. I knew I was literally being taken for a ride and that I shouldn't let him get away with it.

'Now Johnston', I said to myself, 'you're not the woman I think you are if you don't do something about this.'

As we eventually pulled up outside my friend's house I gathered up all my bags and papers. Everything in me just wanted to pay the fare, which was by this time about sixteen pounds plus, and get into the house, where I would presumably moan to all and sundry about how he had duped me, and fantasize about what I *could* have said. In my heart, though, the onus was on me to deal with it now. Summoning all my theatrical technique I presented myself at his window as 'woman in control of situation'. I asked for a receipt. He filled it in watching me like a vulture watching its meal. He clutched it to his chest until I handed over the money, plus a very small tip. Don't even ask me why I tipped him, perhaps it was something to do with not wanting to sink to his level or, more practically, that I knew I would never get the receipt if I didn't tip. Or could it be that my assertiveness was already beginning to slip? I then said musingly, 'It's strange that this same journey usually costs eight pounds'.

'You've got to be joking!', scoffed this modern day MacHeath.

'No I'm not joking', I replied icily, 'but just in case there has been a mistake, I've taken your number and tomorrow, when I've made the same journey again, and checked the route, I'll contact your company and we will compare the prices.' He gawped as I turned on my heel. It was going well; though my heart was pounding, I looked cool enough. I set off across the pavement towards the house, with my bags and papers gathered to me. And then I fell over.

Flat out on the pavement, papers and bags flying in the wind and scattering all around me, I grovelled around collecting my 'bits', trying desperately not to look undignified. But with two big holes in my tights and blood running down my legs, I didn't think I was succeeding. 'Don't cry, don't cry', I was screaming inside my head. I stood up intact. The enemy was still sitting in his cab, the engine ticking.

'Thank you for asking, but no I'm fine', I said haughtily, and gathering all my dignity – about an eighth-of-an-inch – I left the scene.

Is it, then, a question of 'once a mess always a mess'? I'm sure I'll always be a little bit messy, but I'm never afraid to admit it. And on the day I met Clare Short I realized that I had held on to the 'messy times'. And they have made me grow. I've got a lot of growing still to do, but I hope that one day, out of the mess, I'll be 'good enough'.